SEO

A Layman's Guide

Robb Wallace

AF808885

ROBB WALLACE .CO.UK

Robb Wallace Media

CONTENTS

Chris Wain: Unique Adventure Tours Scotland

As a web developer and designer, I found Robb's take on the web and SEO refreshing rather than intimidating, giving me a way to learn, understand and develop my own skills and knowledge, while expanding my understanding of what it takes to grow my online business.

Having now set up an adventure tour company based on my 20 year experience as an adventure activity guide and tour developer (consolidating all my skills into one business).

I had some fantastic tours in some of the most scenic locations in Scotland, partnerships with some of the best chef's and hotels but what I needed was customers – Robb helped my business become a reality.

Just building a website and having a few social media pages are not enough anymore – you need Robb (all be it in printed form) to help you compete, find your voice, and get in front of the right people.

Helping to take my online business presence to the next level, compete proactively, to ultimately engage and attract visitors/potential clients, Robb's book SEO: A layman's guide helped me turn my website & social media channels into productive team players in my small business empire, using a combination of elements to build up written and visual content to grow and develop my reach and ultimately my client base.

I can whole heartedly say that without Robb and the knowledge his book shares, my business would still be lost in the sandpit at the end of the internet, the proof is throughout my digital footprint and online products.

Chris Wain

Owner & Operator (Sole Trader)

Unique Adventure Tours Scotland

https://www.uniqueadventuretoursscotland.co.uk

1

WHY SEO? GOOD QUESTION

SEO or Search Engine Optimisation is the dark art of ticking boxes to make sure that all the work you have put into 1: Making your website and 2: The product or information hosted on said website actually gets traffic. SEO is applying the best of the widely acknowledged industry standards and practices to your website. Why? To give your website the best chance of ranking when a potential client or customer goes looking for the valued information hosted within your website. This is why we dedicated time and effort to search engine optimisation.

Now if you were to ask "*What You Must Know to Rank Your Website Higher with SEO*" to an AI (Artificial Intelligence) writing software, which essentially scans the web, does its research and then rewrites what it finds. It would spit out something like this.

-What is SEO & why it's important?

SEO is the abbreviation for Search Engine Optimisation. It is a process which helps a website to rank high up in search engine result pages. SEO optimises content so that it can be found by people who are looking for it or topics related to it.

SEO is important because it helps in drawing traffic to your website and making people aware of your brand and products. It also helps in improving the ranking of your website on search engines like Google, Bing, Yahoo etc.

The process of SEO starts from keyword research, keyword optimisation, backlink building and other strategies for improving rankings on SERP's.

-The process of Search Engine Optimisation

Search engine optimisation is the process of affecting the visibility of a website or a web page in a search engine's unpaid results.

SEO is essential for digital marketing to succeed. It is not only important when it comes to organic reach, but also for paid campaigns. SEO can be done through various methods that are either in-house or outsourced by an agency.

-The Do's and Don'ts of SEO. What you should know.

This article is meant for people who are new to SEO. It covers the basics of SEO and what you should know before you start optimizing your website.

The first thing to know is that SEO is not a one-time investment. It takes time and it requires patience. The success or failure of your site depends on it. You need to be serious about it because if you don't follow these steps, Google will penalize you by ranking your site lower than it should be according to its merits.

If you want your site to rank higher in the SERPS (Search Engine Results Page), then the do's are: 1) publish quality content; 2) build backlinks; 3) optimise for mobile devices; 4) use keywords in title, description, tags & content

-Tips to rank higher on Google and other search engines

There are many factors that determine how high a website will rank on search engines but the main two are content and links.

Content:

In order to rank higher, the content must be well researched and organised so it can be easily understood. The content should have good grammar and a clear voice. It is also important to write about topics that are relevant to your target audience.

Links:

The more links you have, the higher your ranking will be because it tells Google that people are linking to your site therefore they trust what you post in your blog or website. Linking out to other sites also gives them the opportunity for reciprocal link building where they link back to you in return.

Everything the AI spat out in seconds is relevant and covers some of the basics but there is so much more to SEO. We will look deeper.

This comes from Rytr - Check it out here >> https://robb.link/rytr

NOTE: AI content creators like RYTR are great for churning out the first draft of content on a chosen topic, but make sure you rework it for the intended audience.

Google Is Search.

In the words of Google.

> "Our mission is to organise the world's information and make it universally accessible and useful. *People around the world turn to Search to find information, learn about topics of interest, and make important decisions. We know that people rely on us, so our commitment will never*

waver. As technology evolves, we will continue to help everyone find the information that they're looking for. We believe Search should: Deliver the most relevant and reliable information available."

https://www.google.com/intl/en_uk/search/howsearchworks/mission/
Understand this and you will understand what needs to be done to succeed online.

How does Ranking Work?

A classic joke in SEO used to be "Where is the best place to hide a dead body?", and the punchline was "Page two of Google". Why? Because no one goes there! Nothing ever stands still, and this is especially true for the technology of the internet and search. These are some of the fastest moving technologies of our generation. So I took the liberty to update the joke. A better answer for today's search would be either "Just beyond the Google featured post/snippet" or "Halfway down page one" because no one even scrolls that far anymore. Why? Because people want the information they are seeking and they want it fast, combined with a trust or cultural acceptance that Google, the all-knowing tech god has filtered through the unworthy and delivered the best results in the correct order. We inherently trust the machine!

In this book, I am going to show you lots of different ways to understand SEO and highlight a number of the parts that make up the whole. I am going to break down how to understand and analyse your website and what to change and why, all with the goal to make your website more competitive. This will allow your website to grow naturally and climb up the Google rankings over time. This is not instant rankings, for instant traffic to your website use Google Ads.

It is interesting to note that only twenty-five years ago there was no SEO industry, as there was no internet. However, as the internet grew and companies like Google rose to the challenge of indexing the internet, the dark arts (Dark Arts = done by few behind closed doors) rose to manipulate the search results being returned by Google and other search providers. Fast forward twenty or so years and Google is one of the most sophisticated high tech companies in the world. In a fraction of a second, they take your search query and return a series of results in a ranked fashion. Each one of the hundreds of thousands of websites that match your search query has been ranked by over 200 different factors and all this happens almost instantaneously before Google returns the results we see.

In the book "In the Plex: How Google Thinks, Works, and Shapes Our Lives by Steven Levy " a book about Google's history and growth, it is extremely clear that a key driving factor in everything Google does is SPEED. And Yes, speed is a major ranking factor and something we will look at later.

The Future is AEO

AEO, I.E. *Answer Engine Optimisation*. Because modern Google is essentially an answer engine, it is no longer just a search function in an extensive index. It is a living and breathing intelligence that answers anything and everything you throw at it. Maybe we should rename it? Just a thought.

This SEO Book.

This book is broken into chapters and at first, it may appear strange. For example, the first real chapter is on customer experience and not technical SEO or Keywords. This is because I am writing this book as 1: A layman's guide, to provide a solid overview of many of the factors that contribute to a great website and great SEO and 2: This is almost the exact blueprint/information I use when analysing clients websites to see where we can make improvements to start outranking their competition. So read through all the chapters, take notes, download the plugins, software, check out the links etc and get ready to transform your website.

Oh and once you have read the book, please leave a review!

Ok, one last thing, before we start, jump on your computer, load up Google's chrome browser and search for ***SEO Meta one click*** or click the link below and add it to your chrome browser. I refer to it a lot. https://chrome.google.com/webstore/detail/seo-meta-in-1-click/bjogjfinolnhfhkbipphpdlldadpnmhc

1* Note: If you are looking for instant ranking and exposure you need a book on Google adverts, SEO is a slow route to traffic but if you build they will come.

2* Note: *Full disclosure* https://robb.link/... indicates a link to affiliate products. These are products that I use for SEO. Products that I believe in hence reaching out to secure affiliate links for them. Purchasing any of these products doesn't not effect the price you pay, but it will kick back a small amount to me. Thank you if you subscribe to any of these products via my affiliate links. Much appreciated.

2

Information Sheet

The information sheet (can also be used for clients) is the key information you need to collect before you can start your SEO journey. Some of the information will be on hand, other information will need some research, however some information like keywords etc can be refined later as you work your way through the book.

Business Name and Slogan:

Business Categories/Niches:

Business Address, Email, Phone:

Service area/location:

Website URL:

Social Media Channels - Please indicate most important:

Target Keywords for each page: - Indicate page URL and keywords:

Target Customers, Demographic etc:

Main Product or Service:

Competitors including Website:

Business Goals:

3

CUSTOMER EXPERIENCE

If you have searched online or dabbled a little you will know that SEO is to do with keywords, alt tags, header tags etc. This is true and we will get to that, but as Google evolves and as the customer or end-user becomes accustomed to a high level of daily internet usage, the key thing becomes *Customers Experience*. There are many metrics that report customer experience to Google. This is then fed into Google's special sauce to determine the value of your website when returning results. Having a great customer experience is good for SEO. Think of SEO as digital *word of mouth* or online *word of mouth*. Your SEO depends on building a great site for Google and a great site for your humans. Succeed in both and your rankings will rise. Why start with customer experience in an SEO book? Simple, this is where the customer will start, when they land on your website. The rest of the book is dedicated to getting the customers to your website.

Basic Terms

Website: Refers to your entire website.

Homepage: This is the main page of your website, the main landing page.

Page: Refers to any of the many pages that populate a website.

Post: This refers to the pages that make up your blog.

Mobile Site - The World Is Now Mobile First!

Everyone owns a mobile phone, not everyone owns a desktop or laptop computer. Google thinks about a mobile first website and so should you. This is evidenced in 1: Google's secret UX (User Experience) guides 2: In Google's various tools for analysing website speed. Google's page speed tool used to display the desktop score first but now it shows the mobile scores first, a subtle indicator that Google is now mobile first. 3: Everyone owns a mobile!

https://growrevenue.io/secret-google-ux-playbooks/ (make on RW)

https://developers.google.com/speed/pagespeed/insights

Desktop Second

A mass of small business websites are made by marketeers, and or graphic designers. Most graphic designers who make websites still think in large 16 by 9 style landscape layouts for websites. Why? Because they work on a desktop PC or Mac with large landscape orientated displays, eight plus hours a day! So if you have had a graphics designer make your website, make sure that it is mobile ready. i.e. it is a responsive design that resizes to all viewing devices.

Think mobile first, desktop second. Designing for a desktop with extensive use of images, widgets and horizontal space is a sure-fire way to stop moving with the times and reduce your capacity to compete. Make sure you have a great mobile experience and a great desktop experience for your customers.

Overall Look And Feel?

When it comes to SEO; and websites we are all in the same game. i.e. getting folks to our websites and getting them to buy/interact/share etc from our websites. One of the largest barriers to this is the *look, feel & function* of a website. Take five minutes to look at your competitors, look at the best websites in your general sector and see what they are doing well. Be it colour, button placement, call to action, headlines, video, speed etc and assess your website in comparison. Be brutal, the customer will be. A website straight out of the 90's that doesn't resize, and looks like the 90's will see your potential customers bounce right back to Google. If they aren't happy with the look, the content or aren't able to find or navigate to the content they need, they will return to Google. My threshold is about 4 seconds! Others may have lower thresholds. Be honest, if a website is not delivering, how long do you wait before returning to Google? For design inspiration check the Google playbook.

https://growrevenue.io/secret-google-ux-playbooks/

Above The fold

Above the fold or before you scroll. This is the first thing you see as the website loads up. i.e the the first visual experience! It should grab the attention of the user and deliver. Do not miss this opportunity to deliver. For the homepage, this should include everything from contact information, book now buttons, newsletter sign up, clear navigation, and a clear message of what it is your website offers. Whatever you deem the utmost importance to your customer/user, should be above the fold. For an individual page, it could be the feature list, emotive call to action, problem that you solve, header or title, an image, booking button, download link, sign up form, whatever they are expecting. These rules apply equally to mobile and desktop.

Colours

Colours have so many unconscious cultural associations, so choose wisely if you veer away from white. Most of the largest and most expensive websites in the world, made by the biggest companies in the world use a simple white background with a dark grey or black text. This works. If it is good enough for Google, Apple, Microsoft, Facebook etc then it is good enough for me. I would avoid anything that makes it harder for you customer to read, view etc. Whichever colours you choose for images, background and text, make sure to contrast them well. **Note:** 1 in 12 males are colour blind and the largest group have a red/green/brown complication, so it is best to avoid these combinations of colours on your page.

These websites will keep you right when it comes to colour schemes in relation to accessibility issues and contrast.

https://coolors.co/contrast-checker

https://www.w3.org/WAI/perspective-videos/contrast/

Relevant Headlines And Page Copy

Headlines are crucial for SEO, as is page copy (words on the page), however from a user experience they are just as crucial. If you have offered in your SERP (the small snippet of text that appears in the Google result) **Alien being found alive.** When the customer arrives on-page and sees that the headline was just click bait, with no substance they will drop you like a hot potato and so will Google. Your headlines and your copy should always be of value. Google receives a query from a customer, it decides on the best results and serves them. It wants to serve the customer the best result every time, with the most relevant information to the original search as possible. If your headers are just click bait and your content is weak and of no value, Google will demote it. Provide value.

Jargon Acronyms And Marketeer Talk

So many industries nowadays are full of marketeer talk and experts making themselves look and sound important by the overuse of industry-specific jargon and acronyms. If it needs to be there, then yes, use them but at least explain them. But if it is just superfluous bull shit, then cut it. Users want information, they want clear communication that gets straight to the point. If the customer doesn't know what is being said, you guessed it, they are on their way back to the search results.

Professional Branding

First impressions matter, you could have some of the best material online, but a potential customer sees your 1980's Microsoft paint style logo and goes straight back to Google. A logo can be a simple affair. Make sure you have one that is consistent across your various online spaces and looks professional.

https://www.creativebloq.com/graphic-design/pro-guide-logo-design-21221

User-Friendly Navigation

Being able to navigate anywhere on the website is key, if a customer knows you sell books but can't find them, then they ain't buying them. Having a logical hierarchy to your sites navigation is key to good navigation. Note: for your mobile website, make sure that your buttons, especially your navigation and menu buttons are fat finger-friendly. Another thing to note on website menus and navigation is persistent headers, persistent headers are always located at the top or button of a page and no matter where you scroll they stay there. This is great because it allows the user access to the menu and easy navigation from anywhere on your site, without having to scroll back to the top of the page.

Booking / Contact

If contact information is key to the way you operate your business it should be in a key place and easily accessible. It should have a 'click to call' button, and or 'click to email', 'click to message'. If you're using a contact form, use a form that displays well on both desktop and mobile, make sure it is fat finger friendly and make sure it lets the customer know that their form/query has been sent. Take time to make sure your forms work, that they are sent to the right email, that any sequence etc is firing correctly. And always reply in due course, if you've made a promise of 24hrs then make sure you reply within 24hrs. Manage the customer's expectations and deliver.

HTML code. Just add a "<" before the a on each line.

a href="tel:12345678">Call us at 123-456-789

a href="mailto: abc@example.com">Send Email

a href="url">link text

Chat

Instant chat on websites can be powerful. AI-powered instant chat platforms are used by some of the largest online retailers, however, if you don't have the budget for a big AI chat client to be integrated to your website, think about integrating the social media channel you use most. Like what's app or Facebook messenger. If using instant chat, be aware that customers are expecting an instant reply, not a contact form, so if you can't facilitate it, don't. However, if you do include chat to a social channel do not install it onto your website, just add it as a 'click to open' feature as this will reduce page weight (more later). And page weight is directly linked to page speed. So always weigh up the potential benefits with the potential negatives.

An interesting chat option is Frase and their answer bot. Their AI scans your website and is then ready to answer customers chat questions based on the information on your website. Clever.

https://robb.link/Frase

Forms

I briefly touched on forms earlier, the key thing is to make them responsive, make them fat finger-friendly, make them work. It is a fairly simple formula, but I can't tell you how many forms on customers websites I have tested that were broken. This could be down to software updates, poor setup, no setup, no testing etc. Give the customer a good experience make sure your forms work.

Responsive Design - Desktop, Laptop, Tablet, Smartphones + Multiple browsers

By now this should be self-explanatory, potential customers will be accessing your website from multiple devices. Make sure that your website displays well on all key devices, iPhone, Android phones and tablets, as well as laptops and desktops. Also check it on the key browsers i.e. Chrome, Safari, Edge, Opera, Firefox, Brave. Use the website below to see how your website displays on different virtual devices.

https://responsivedesignchecker.com/

Relevant Use Of Images

Images have weight, so use them sparingly. For user experience make sure your images are optimised, i.e. the image file is compressed, no one has time to wait ten minutes whilst a raw 48MPX image with a file size of 24MB downloads. Compress your images, (lower the quality) speed is king.

Images should complement your website, they should convey whatever it is you are conveying, they should add value to the customer and be used to highlight or emphasise key items visually. A common mistake desktop first designed websites make is a horizontal stack of images, which looks great on desktop but when a mobile browser views it, the horizontal stack becomes a vertical stack and when accessed on mobile the user, has to scroll through lots of unoptimised images to get to any information. That is not a good customer experience.

Relevant Use Of Video

Video can be extremely powerful. It is a great way to convey information about a product or service, give testimonials or reviews and more. However, video can be deployed badly. It can be embedded in code that's old (Iframes) and does not allow it to resize on mobile. Make sure your videos resize. Another problem with video is they add a lot to page weight, which ultimately slows down website loading times, providing a bad user experience. You can speed this up by only loading a thumbnail of the video when the customer arrives, not the whole video and then load the video when they click the thumbnail. Look for a *video lightbox pop up* and *lazy load* to facilitate this.

Readable Font

Having great content in a font that no one can read will destroy your customer experience. Stick to the basics and make them clear and legible.

Grammar And Spelling

It may not matter to you, but it will matter to your customers. There are now so many tools available to assist you as you type. Make sure you don't look unprofessional by having simple spelling and grammar mistakes sprinkled throughout your content.

https://www.grammarly.com/

https://robb.link/ProWritingAid

Social Media Access

If having a solid community around your website is key then make accessing and sharing your content on social media easy. Common practice is to have links to your social media profiles in the header and footer and "share now" buttons under each article or item for ease of sharing. Make it as easy as possible for someone excited about your content to share it. No one is going to go out of their way to copy the URL etc, if it is not as easy as a single click, it ain't getting shared.

Custom 404 Page

When someone is directed to the wrong page or mistypes the URL they are directed to a 404 page. The worst kind of 404 page is a blank abyss. Creating a custom 404 page can allow you to create some humour around the error and give the potential customers some options of how to get back to the content they were looking for. This is another reason for having a persistent menu bar on your website, as no matter where they go they can navigate to the next place.

https://www.creativebloq.com/web-design/best-404-pages-812505

Pop-Ups And Other Annoying Anomalies.

This chapter is about user experience and how the customer interacts with your website, it is about giving them an experience worthy of them buying, coming back, leaving a review, telling their friends about you. Popups are annoying. Be honest with yourself, some popups we will tolerate, like a subtle notification popup for cookies or GDPR but a large popup for your email or some spam advert that you can't click off for the "X" is so hidden, that it takes you a few seconds to work out where it is. These are sure-fire ways to leave a bad impression. Popups, adverts, auto-playing videos, auto-playing audio, the key is to be aware of your audience and treat them as you would like to be treated. Think like a customer.

Freshness - Website, Blogs etc

When was the last time your website was updated? For some websites, this is far more important than others, but for most who are selling something or providing information etc then freshness is important. Everything from the information being presented, to the look and feel of the website, to the underlying technologies and software the website is running on should be updated regularly. If you're offering a product or service and your above the fold image is still advertising Halloween, one week before Christmas, it will not fill the customer with confidence that their goods will be sent out etc. News sites with no new content. Wrong opening times. Wrong prices, etc. Take time to update your website regularly.

Website Languages

If your customers base is multilingual then make sure you offer up the option for a native language selection. This is fairly easy to do on most website software.

Accessibility

There can be many reasons why some can't access your website, auditory, visual cognitive, physical and more reasons why. Everyone should be able to access your website and the more accessible it is, the more potential customers you may have. Making your website accessible can help boost brand recognition by showing your customers that you care and that you're making efforts to make your website inclusive. If you are a very large website it can also safeguard you from lawsuits, making sure you're complying with legislation. There are many plugins to plug and play accessibility features like increasing the size of text, changing the contrast of text, reading out the alt tags of images and more. More in the accessibility section.

https://blog.hubspot.com/website/wordpress-accessibility-plugin

Favicon

This is the small icon that is displayed in the tab of the browser when you are on a website, Google has a small G, Apple displays their brand etc. It doesn't really serve a purpose but it is a part of the branding and overall professional feel of a website, if your website doesn't have one, the subconscious mind might ask why not? and automatically not trust the website. Our brains take in way more information than we give them credit for. Upload a favicon to your website.

Green Padlock

The green padlock is displayed at the top left next to the domain name. This is represented by 'https' in the URL and indicates that the website is secure and instils trust, especially on an ecommerce website.

Cookies/GDPR

Legislation in certain countries states that you need to indicate tracking info and what it is being used for. If your customers are expecting a popup for this and they don't get one, it can be a red flag to the legitimacy of the website. Chapter 11 for all the info you need on this.

4

KEYWORDS

Keywords are the *Key* i.e. the main words that you will attempt to rank for. These words are at the core of the page and at the core of the content. These can be a single word, sentence, topic cluster or phrase.

See What's There Already.

For any page, on the web navigate to your tool bar and click on the chrome extension SEO Meta One Click > Tools Tab > *Analyse keyword density with Mtips*, then click analyse.

or go straight to https://www.wmtips.com/tools/keyword-density-analyzer/

This page will show you at a glance all the keywords and groupings of words for any page on your website or a competitors website. This tool is a great way to research the keywords already on your website and then later to find the keywords related to your main keyword.

Top Tip: To find multiple keywords related to your main keyword use Wikipedia. Go to Wikipedia and type in the main keyword. i.e Brazilian Jiu Jitsu, click on the page, now click on SEO Meta > Tools Tab > *Analyse keyword density with Mtips*, then click analyse. As Wikipedia has so much depth and covers almost all aspects of a topic on one page, the keywords returned here are a goldmine of similar and associated keywords. Look through these keywords to get ideas for words you are missing from your page. Thank me later with a review!

Keywords You Rank For.

Before we look at keywords any further we need to understand what keywords you are currently ranking for. You can use software like SerpStat and SERanking to see what words your website ranks for and then track those words over time. To see which words you rank for without tracking you can use *Google Search Console*. Once you plug your domain into your software of choice you will be able to see how many words you are currently ranking for. These ranking software's allow you to select Google search engine locations, which is important as ranking changes due to location. So I can set the ranking for Glasgow or Scotland, or the UK or the USA to target how Google is ranking my website for specific keywords in the location of my audience. It can also be a surprise to see what words from your website rank and what words do not.

https://Appsumo.com is a great marketplace for entrepreneurs and frequently has great deals on SEO software including keyword ranking software. Use the link **http://fbuy.me/v/robbwallacemedia_1** to get $10 off your first Appsumo purchase.

Google Search Console: Linking your website to *Google search console* allows you to see which search queries are bringing people to your website and which of those are being clicked. This is a great free option to get started with and a must for every website.

Manual: Open up a privacy browser in anonymous mode. (Google your browser) I recommend Brave or Epic but most browsers have a privacy function. Now search the keywords you would expect your website to rank for. Make a list of the rankings, some may be well beyond page one.

Paid options (Affiliate Links)
https://robb.link/SERPstat
https://robb.link/SEranking

Free options:
https://search.google.com/search-console/about
https://smallseotools.com/keyword-position/
https://www.seobility.net/en/rankingcheck/
https://app.neilpatel.com/en/ubersuggest
https://www.spyfu.com

Keyword Research

Once we have an idea of the words we are either ranking for or the words which we would like to rank for, we have to think about the different ways in which people will use that word or phrase to search with it. Words are powerful in SEO. If I am selling a "BJJ Journal" I want to look at all the ways I can say that, and find all the ways a potential customer may type or speak that request into Google.

I.e.

Brazilian Jiu Jitsu Journal, Brazilian Jiu Jitsu Notepad, Brazilian Jiu Jitsu Manual, Brazilian Jiu Jitsu books, Brazilian Jiu Jitsu training Journal, Brazilian Jiu Jitsu Diary, BJJ Journal, BJJ Notepad, BJJ Manual, BJJ books, BJJ training Journal, BJJ Diary. Then look at all the questions around this like *"Will a bjj diary help my game?"*, or *"What is the best jiu jitsu training journal?"* etc etc leave no stone unturned! One of the very best ways to see what people are searching for in relation to your keyword or phrase is to type it into Google and see what Google's auto suggestion brings up, or scroll to the bottom of the first page and see the similar search feature provided by Google. This is the most accurate, as it is Google telling you directly what is being searched for around your keyword or phrase.

Keyword research is about understanding your target keywords, your competitor's keywords, keyword search volumes, variations and questions around your keyword and how competitive your keyword is. The key is to create valuable content using as many variations of the keyword and potential questions as possible into your page. I also use websites like *Answer The Public, Keyword Surfer, SerpStat and Wikipedia* to find more combinations of these words. I also analyse the top websites returned by Google to see what keywords and questions they are using.

Group your keywords together, find topic clusters and expand, expand, expand.

Paid options that I actually use. (These are Affiliate Links)

https://robb.link/SERPstat
https://robb.link/SEranking
https://robb.link/Frase

Free options:

https://keywordshitter.com
https://youautocompleteme.io
https://answerthepublic.com
https://www.keywordtooldominator.com/keyword-tools
https://keywordtool.io
https://www.wordstream.com/keywords

https://chrome.google.com/webstore/detail/seostack-keyword-tool/labjajhkfjfncpiddbgdimcaldgeognn?hl=en

Your Keyword Competition

Check the competition, check which keywords are working well for them. If they have already optimised and are already ranking for said keywords, then you can use these keywords too, as they are all ready proven to drive traffic. You can scan their website with software like SE Ranking, Serpstat and using the SEO Meta One click extension.

Search Volume And Search Competition.

Search volume is a key metric in understanding the weight of the keyword and its importance. Search volume simply indicates how many searches per month any given keyword has in Google. These will vary from location to location. This allows us to make decision about the importance of particular keyword choice.

If "Rafting Scotland" receives 140 searches per month and "White Water Rafting Scotland" receives 720 searches per month then I can assume that "White Water Rafting Scotland" will potentially be harder to rank to No1 than "Rafting Scotland", which by comparison should be relatively easy. Why? Because an increase in search volume usually means increase in search competition but this is not always true. And finding high volume keywords that have low competition is a great way to build your content. These are often called "low hanging fruit".

As high search volume usually indicates a higher competition in keywords, we must chose our battles when choosing keywords. This is where you choose your battles, taking on a keyword that is too competitive will sap your energy and time with little to no result. For example attempting to secure listing for "Samsung Phones" with a search volume of 90,500 in the UK or something similar with a ridiculously high search volume would be inadvisable but trying to secure, "How to reset a Samsung Phone" which has 1,600 searches per month will be a lot more attainable. Get specific, know your audience and understand the search volume and search competition of the keywords your going after.

Paid options (Affiliate Links)

https://robb.link/SERPstat

https://robb.link/SEranking

Free Options

https://chrome.google.com/webstore/detail/keyword-surfer/bafijghppfhdpldihckdcadbcobikaca

Gives you search volume directly in the Google search bar. Great for Keyword research.

https://ads.google.com/intl/en_uk/home/tools/keyword-planner/

Googles own keyword tool, gives accurate volume searches. Part of a Google ads account.

Keyword Ideas And Suggestions.

Generating lots and lots of keywords that are associated with your keyword is the key to keyword success, for it gives you an idea of the many ways in which people will search your keyword.

There are sites like *Answer The Public* etc that will give you multiple questions around the keyword of choice, however using the following will all help you build new keyword suggestions to test; using a thesaurus, Google's auto complete search function, Google's auto complete suggestions, as well as niche forums related to the keyword, Facebook groups, hashtag searches on social media.

i.e BJJ. We could look at Google's auto complete and BJJ user forums, Facebook groups, BJJ websites and get words like *Grappling, wrestling, MMA, Judo, Combat sports, Gi, No Gi, black belt, training, competition, IBJJF, Gordon Ryan.*

In this example I am looking for as many keywords as possible that are in some way associated with or interchangeable with the keyword BJJ. So I look for other names for it, look at the clothing and training apparatus associated with it, brands. I look at the different styles, different grades, the history, the biggest stars and social media influencers, why people would do it? What are the alternatives? Why is it better or worse? etc etc and make a big list of both short and long tail keywords. I then go in and check the search volume and competition for each one of these. From there I decide which keywords to work on. Am I going to go hard and try to compete for the most dominant words and phrases or am I going to attack the low lying fruit and tackle the low volume keywords? To be fair I usually do both, as I want all the keywords covered! Every keyword you research will have an associated niche related to it, it will be vast and offer great ideas.

Short Tail

A short tail keyword is just that short. It is usually the main word or words in a long tail keyword. I.e. BJJ but as BJJ is at the route of many long tail keywords and questions, ranking for just "BJJ" as single keyword is going to be hard unless your website is dedicated to BJJ and nothing else for years. Most likely it will be a large governing body, Wikipedia, a news outlet or something similar that will have the short tail keyword secured.

Long Tail

BJJ training Diary, what is the best BJJ training diary, Who is the best BJJ player? These are all good examples of long tail keywords. As they are more specific in their statement, there will be far less people searching for it and therefore easier to secure. So long tail keywords tend to cover all of your main short tail keywords in a sentence, question or statement.

Keywords And Headers

Every page of a website has header tags. Header tags within a website page, are weighted between H1 and H6, where H1 is of most importance and most weight. Headers tell Google what the main focus of a page is about, breaking up the content in terms of importance. Using your main keywords in your H1 and then using variations of your keywords and long tail keywords in your H2, H3, H4, H5, H6 tags. Whilst still creating engaging content, full of value.

Download and install SEO Meta 1 click, which is my favourite chrome extension, it is so versatile. Then navigate to your homepage. Open a new tab and navigate to your competitors homepage. On each page click on SEO Meta 1 click and go to the second tab and check the headers. The H1 tag should be about the main longtail keyword being targeted, then the H2s etc should be about variations of this keyword. Compare your headers to that of the competition, this is a great way to analyse a competitors page.

https://chrome.google.com/webstore/detail/seo-meta-in-1-click/bjogjfinolnhfhkbipphpdlldadpnmhc

Example from my website, I have one H1 and lots of H2s. Each of these H2s has a paragraph about the main topic, which is represented in the Header i.e. the H1 tag. I am clearly telling Google that this page is about improving your BJJ game with use of a journal. more on Header tags later.

https://www.robbwallace.co.uk/books/jiu-jitsu-training-journal-diary-log-notebook/

H1 Jiu Jitsu Training Journal Diary Log Notebook
H2 Take your BJJ game to the next level.
H2 JIU-JITSU TRAINING DIARY
H3 With over 150 training sessions per book, our bjj diaries offer exceptional value for money at only £7.99 UK or $9.99 US
H2 Jiu-jitsu training Journal
H2 The secret to great Brazilian Jiu jitsu
H2 Contents of the Jiu-Jitsu Planner (Training Journal)
H2 Key Benefits of our Jiu Jitsu Journal
H2 Jiu Jitsu Training Planner Videos
H2 Why create a Jiu Jitsu training diary?
H2 A journal for every jiu jitsu belt.
H2 Jiu Jitsu is complicated
H2 What is Brazilian jiu-jitsu?
H2 What is the difference between Brazilian jiu jitsu and other martial arts?
H2 What is the history of Brazilian jiu-jitsu?
H2 What are the benefits of Brazilian jiu jitsu?
H2 How long does it take to learn Brazilian jiu-jitsu?
H2 Take action today and skyrocket your jiu-jitsu game!!
H2 Jiu Jitsu Journal Video Stories

Ranking

To understand your ranking in Google, you need some way of tracking the keyword in particular locations (Google UK, Google USA etc) over time. Purchasing a rank tracking software will allow you to track the most important keywords for your project over time and is a must for SEO. As the months go by, and the work is being done you will see your keywords rank higher and higher. It will also allow you to see keywords that are not working or need work. Again Appsumo is a great place to secure life time deals on SEO software.

Paid options (Affiliate Links)

https://robb.link/SERPstat

https://robb.link/SEranking

Keyword Cloud

A keyword header cloud generator like Nibbler allows you to see at a glance, the main keywords within a websites homepage. Which is good to quickly identify the target keywords of a website in the eyes of Google or a similar bot, that scans websites. If you scan one of your website pages with this tool and see that all your keywords are not related to the main topic of the page or its highlighting something like your email address, or a buy now button, then it can let you know at a glance if an aspect of your SEO is off. ie your *Header Tag* assignment. The same goes for when you scan your pages and look at the header tags with Meta one click. If it shows you ten H1s that say email or something else random, then you need to fix this.

https://nibbler.silktide.com

https://www.wmtips.com/tools/keyword-density-analyzer/

Keyword Stuffing

Back in the good old days keyword stuffing was super effective. In fact many folks would ram the entire page full, and every empty space had keywords stuffed. In fact I used to stuff keywords in the same colour font as the background, invisible to the humans but clear as day to Google. These were only visible to Googles spiders, but now a days Google is super clever, ever evolving and all knowing, so keyword stuffing is no longer a viable option. So don't over stuff your pages. Content is king, give value and they will come.

5

GROWTH OPTIMISATION

Tools To Capture The Customer And Sales

In this section, we will look at some of the key items that will keep the customer's focus and give them a great experience, as well as maximising your website's potential. Why is this relevant to SEO? Again it comes down to digital word of mouth. When your website is working and delivering the goods, more folk will be satisfied with the experience and will talk about it, share it, leave reviews etc and Google will notice it and rank it higher.

Homepage

Your homepage is essentially just an index, it's a landing page that allows people to get to the right page. I do not want to make my home page so powerful that it out ranks my product pages for their specific keywords. Your homepage should only rank for your brand and your general categories, let the rest of your pages rank for specific keywords related to your products or services.

Prominent Contact Info - Phone, Email, Messenger

If your business demands it make sure it is accessible to everyone who makes the journey to your website. Add in the 'click to call' HTML to make it super easy for them to contact you. This comes into its own on a phone as the code will access the phones call, email or chat functionality automatically. i.e. When you are surfing a website on your phone and click the phone number it will open your dial app, ready to call the number.

Location Address And Map.

For a business with a physical location have your address shown prominently in the classic NAP (Name, Address, Phone consistency) format and a map link to Google or Apple maps. This can either show the map (extra page weight) or it can be a click to access Google maps or click to access Apple maps. This allows customers again, to easily access the location on their phone as a satnav.

Call To Action (CTA or C2A)

A call to action is your way to tell the customer to take action. It's a classic sales pitch of *Problem, Solution, C2A.*

Problem: Your website is not performing as you dreamed it should.

Solution: SEO a layman's guide.

C2A: Buy a copy today and start transforming your website tomorrow.
Buy now at Robbwallace.co.uk

Make sure you are using a call to action throughout your pages.

How You Help The Customer.

Regardless the nature of your website, if it is only accessible to nuclear physicists with IQs of 500,000 then it's going to flop. Clearly define how you assist your audience and what you are doing for them. This is also a great place to define your broad keywords, short and long tail that define your customers and their concerns as well as your products and services.

The Problems You Solve - Is It Clear?

What problems are you solving? Have you defined it? Are you letting your website visitor know or is it all just a bit vague? If you sell adventures in Scotland then let them know that is the case. For example https://www.uniqueadventuretoursscotland.co.uk lets their customers know that if they are looking for a unique, luxury, adventure in Scotland where everything is done for them then look no further. They're solving the lack of luxury adventure problem, offering bespoke high-end adventures matched with the best accommodation, food and travel. And because he has took the time to understand the market and his audience he can better chose the content, keywords and visuals that will best cater for them.

As well as books, I also sell journals. My selection of journals are solving the problems related to my passions, from dreams, health, gratitude, BJJ, MMA, forgetting passwords and more. Journals to help make the burden of life easier. What ever it is you do clearly define it and then road test it. Don't be scared to follow up with customers and ask them about their experience and then refine.

Unique Selling Proposition (USP)

What makes you different from the competition? Let your visitors know. This is a powerful way to keep customers on your page. Knowing that your solution is unique in the marketplace. This will let them know that more Googling is not required.

Lead Capture Forms

A popular way to capture potential client's details before contacting them is to offer or upsell your solution. i.e. Fill in this form to receive a free 5 minute video assessing your website. You then have their details and their interest. Again, make it fat finger-friendly, make it responsive to device size and make it relevant. If you're offering a free book or free report or discount code etc then make good on your promise and don't go over the top in the number of details you require. Also, filling in a lead capture form is not an invite to spam city.

What Is Done With The Leads?

Following on from the last point, what do you do with the leads? Do you a system in place to capture the details, log the contact details or an automatic system to deliver the free PDF's, or an email sequence that gets triggered? Understand why you employed a lead capture form and know how you are using it and how the customer will experience it. This can be great for generating new customers but if mismanaged it can be entering into GDPR territory. So vigorously test any email captures system you employ on your website.

Relevant Trust Factors

Gain the customers trust, with a professional looking website, with good spelling, a professional logo, a green padlock for SSL encryption and security, quality images and video. There are many factors that signal to the unconscious brain that the site is worthy of me typing in my credit card details. On top of these factors, there are key things that can be done to further signal trust in your site.

https://safeweb.norton.com Check any website against Norton's database, Kaspersky and others offer similar services.

https://transparencyreport.google.com/safe-browsing/search?url= Check any website against Google's database

Positioning, Awards, Money-Back Guarantees

This is about signalling early to your website users, the quality you are offering them, be it the inventor of the ... or the Olympic silver medallist at the... or the regional finalist at ... or trained by, or received a PHD in.....

For example, I am an award-winning filmmaker that has shown my adventure films from Scotland to New Zealand and I let people know this when they are reading my book, Smartphone Smart Marketing. When readers get to the sections on video and photography, they know that it's not just waffle, they are getting my award-winning experience condensed into the book.

Another way to build trust and positioning is by showing confidence in your product or service in the form of a money-back guarantee or via a video.

Secondary Call To Actions

If you have a sales-based website selling products, then having a second call to action is always a good idea.

Newsletter Signup.

Newsletters can be a great way to update your customer base with your latest offers, services, industry insight, tips, hacks, blogs, news, coupons, events etc. So if this is something your website, business or brand could do with, add it in. It's also a great way to bring customers to your site regularly. And increased traffic is good SEO.

Thank You Page

If you have a sales process or sign up page. It is always good to have some form of thank you page to thank them for purchasing or signing up. This completes the process and provides excellent customer service.

Testimonials / Reviews On Display

Video testimonials and reviews on display for the customer to see are a powerful form of validating the authenticity and quality of your products and services. It has been shown that testimonials with associated identity (faces) are stronger than just an anonymous quote, and video testimonials are the most influential of all.

Encouragement To Share Content

Having the functionality to share the article, blog, product is one thing. However, I recommend giving a prompt and encouraging your website user to share it if they enjoyed it, share it with their friends etc this may be the nudge they need to do it. Social media shares are powerful SEO components.

Business Brand Ranks On Page #1

The minimum standard for a website is for it to appear on the first page of Google when someone types your brand name, word for word. If your website is not returning you on the first page for your brand name then you need to understand why. This could be due to a number of reasons including how young your site is, whether or not you have done anything to let Google know you exist, wither you have done any SEO. A competitor with the same name with years of history etc. The easiest keywords to rank for is your brand and your homepage for your brand.

What Keywords Rank On Page #1

Once you have done some keyword research etc you can use a keyword tracker, to monitor your keywords as they move up and down in the search. This is extremely useful as you can see the direct results of the work you are putting in. SERP stands for Search Engine Results Page and relates to the small snippets that represent each unique web page in Google's results page. As you track your keywords over time you will see that they eb and flow and sometime rise like a rocket and at other times they may fall of a cliff. This is why we track.

Keywords Getting CTR (click through rate)

Click through rate for keywords is when your tracking software identifies that a particular keyword brought a customer to your website. So this is showing that this keyword, combined with the title and SERP (the small snippet shown in Googles search results) are working well to hook the user via Google to carry on through to your website. I always advise that you study and understand why this keyword, title and SERP is working. If it is possible to replicate the formula for other pages with lots of impression (people saw it) but no click through rate. Click through rate can be analysed via Google Search Console.

Most Impression With NO CTR

Some website pages may have lots and lots of impressions, i.e. folks are typing the keywords and Google is delivering the goods. However, for some reason the SERP and title is not working, another page is or another SERP is winning. In this case you need to type in that keyword and see what is being returned. Look at your SERP and look at the competitions. Are they more direct? Are they offering something that you are not? Do they use better wording? Is their offer better? Is their SERP more enticing? You only get 160 characters to win them over.

Keyword Used In Page Title

The page title is what the page is about, if your target keywords, that you built your entire article or page around is "Why do my socks always disappear" then you need these words in your title. Don't write a tittle like "Another pair bites the dust" etc. Even though that would be a decent title for an article about why socks always disappear, it doesn't work in SEO land. With everything we do we are telling Google and Humans, what our page is about. We do this with keywords and coherent information built around and associated with those keywords.

So always use your long or short keywords in your page title.

Keywords Used In H1 Tags

Again in everything we do we are telling the computer what our article is about, but always keep it relevant and readable for humans. The H1 is used by Googles robots as they scan your page to get a general idea, in a broad sense of what your webpage is about. This is why you need to have your keyword in your H1. It is good practice to have only one H1 per page. This H1 will usually be your page title or article header. i.e. "Why do my socks always disappear" would be the H1.

An optimal page title is where you look over the page you have written for your website and determine if the page title is optimised. I.e. it is an H1 Tag, there is only one H1 tag and it contains the Keywords you are targeting.

Check any page with SEO Meta one click > headers tab to see what the H1 is and if it relates to the actual target audience of the page.

Brand In Page Title

For the *home page* of your website you want to have your brand in the page title and therefore in the H1 header for the page. i.e. *Robb Wallace Author*. On other pages within your website you would be targeting the keywords related to the product or service in your title, not the brand.

Google My Business Claimed (GMB)

Has your GMB been claimed? GMB is especially powerful when competing for local search results. i.e. If you are a gym, café, local shop or local business then securing your GMB and optimising it is essential to securing good ranking for your business. More covered in the GMB sections.

Local Map Pack Listing

Another SEO joke, well actually it is the same as the last one. Where do you hide a dead body? Just after the map pack listings. If you do a local search for "*local business* near me" and your not one of three options then you probably won't have your website clicked on. Now this is acceptable if the location is not relevant to you, but if the search is and you're not listed then you need to optimise.

Map & Address

Anywhere you're talking about one of your physical locations or a meet up etc, make sure that you include the map and the address. As mentioned earlier you physical address and an active link to the map should be listed in the footer. However, if adding multiple events, for example, for a music gig or author book signings, make it as easy as possible for those people to get the correct information. The maps and addresses are also subtle signals to Google about your real world locations and help with local searches.

Keywords In The Meta Description

As mentioned a few times and to hammer home the idea, get your keywords into your meta description. The meta description is the text tat shows on the Google search page (SERP). For example searching for paddle boarding in Perthshire, this SERP from UATS is returned top on Goggle Scotland. It has locations "Scotland","Perthshire" it has keywords "paddle board", "standup paddle boarding" as well as info about private tours. In the short defined limits of the meta description *Unique Adventure Tours Scotland* has crammed in everything they need to let both Google and the potential customer know what is being offered.

https://www.uniqueadventuretoursscotland.co.uk

Paddle Board Hire & ***Tours*** - Standup ***Paddle Boarding*** in Scotland
Small Private Guided ***Tours*** with Perthshire ***Paddleboarding***.

Blog / Resource Centre

Does your website have a blog? For me and most in the know a blog is one of the best ways to increase your rankings over time. This is simply asking the question, do you have a blog? If you don't, make one. I am talking about a blog that is part of your website. I am not talking about an external blog that hosted on any number of popular blogging sites. Blogs are good for SEO if they are attached to your main site.

More on blogging later.

6

SPEED AND SECURITY

As mentioned earlier speed is one of the key factors in everything Google does, therefore we can assume that speed is a key ranking factor. There is a popular idea that there are over 200 ranking factors but no one really knows how many factors there are and how each is weighted. Everyone who is, is speculating, including me. No on knows the secret Google sauce. But we can speculate, and big studies by MOZ and others have been done and concluded many of the key factors.

Backlinkos list of all 200.
https://backlinko.com/google-ranking-factors
Moz blog detailing the myth of the 200.
https://moz.com/blog/the-myth-of-googles-200-ranking-factors

Google Page Speed

There are many tools to gauge the speed of your website, and we will look at them below. But the key one is Google Page Speed, as its predominantly Google as a search engine that we are looking to "Hack" with our SEO techniques, then we should refer to its own page speed benchmarking tool to see how we fair. The good thing about Google's tool, like most speed benchmarking tools, it gives us a break down of what was good and what needs improved.

So head on over and type in your URL and see how you fare. As this is possibly the first time benchmarking your site, note the score and date and aim to make improvements to increase your speed moving forward.

https://developers.google.com/speed/pagespeed/insights
Or via
SEO Meta > Tools tab

Location Based Speed Tests

Other platforms for bench marking allow you to set the location of your prospective audience. This is great if you have a business or website located in say Scotland that has both a large customer base at home and in the USA. Using these tools will allow you to gauge how fast your website is in your customer's country. This can be down to a number of factors, the main one being server location. If your website is hosted on a server in London and folk from California are accessing your website, then the information has to travel so much further. So having a fast website locally or nationally where your server is located is one thing, making sure it's fast where your customers are based is another.

These tests will show the huge gap in load times across locations. With some locations possibly waiting up to 20 seconds for your website to load. Which is obviously unacceptable to your customer or to Google. Ultimately lowering your ranking.

These tests also show you the other factors that are highlighted below, that will contribute to your websites overall speed. Look at the waterfall diagram and see how your website loads, it is extremely interesting to see how the browser puts your website together and can give you great insight into what needs fixed to deliver a fast customer experience. Improve each, one at a time.

https://tools.pingdom.com

https://gtmetrix.com

https://www.uptrends.com/tools/website-speed-test

Host

Hosting can play such a significant factor in your website's speed and security. The host you choose lays the foundations for what is possible with your website. Does your package offer web hosting, cloud hosting, shared server or solo? Do they have good reviews, good up time, customer service, latest standards, software, security etc.

At a minimum you're looking for a shared server, running on SSD drives with enough bandwidth to allow your traffic to grow. Always double check what your package includes.

After being with many hosts I can recommend Site Ground. Great technical staff, fast servers, and great tools like their caching tool, integration with Cloud flare and Free SSL. Initial discount can be applied to your first purchase for up to three years of hosting.

https://robb.link/SiteGround

Server Location

Server location can be found using *who is* information if you do not know where yours is currently located. Most hosting packages, at purchase give you the facility to select server location. For instance my own website has servers based in the UK as I am an author predominantly based in the UK, writing in British English. However, I do have an equal customer base in the USA and other English speaking nations like Canada, Australia, New Zealand, Ireland etc. So to make sure that my content is delivered to them quickly I use a CDN (*content delivery network*). No one is going to wait 20 seconds for my website to load in Australia.

Who Is Domain

This is a great website for seeing who owns a website, their name, address, server location, host, when the domain was registered, when it expires and more. You can via your host select to display or hide some of these details, especially name, address etc. However, most hosts charge a fee for this service. I use cloud flare to do this for free.

https://who.is

CDN

CDN stands for *content delivery network. I*n layman's terms, a CDN is a network of servers across the world. Each of these servers stores part of your website locally and deliver your website from the nearest location to the website user, speeding up load times and giving them a great user experience. There are a number of solutions available with some host providers including a CDN in there subscription package. Personally, I use Cloudflare as they have a reliable worldwide network and a free option that integrates seamlessly with my host provider Site Ground. If you are working with international clients and serving content across oceans, a CDN is key to fast load times everywhere your end user will access your website.

https://cloudflare.com

https://robb.link/SiteGround

Page Size

Page size is the entire weight of your website. That is all the code and the assets like images, videos, widgets etc. The less page weight you have the less a page has to load and the faster it will load. The first website I built, I thought I needed the best images possible and left the images uncompressed straight from my DSLR camera. I had a page weight of 100MB, and at the time I had no idea why my website was taking 40 plus seconds to load. I thought it was my host and some technical issue! Reduce the size of the code and the assets (images, video etc) to speed up load times. This can be done by compressing images to keep the quality but reduce the size, minifying code to reduce the amount of code, reduce request and so on.

You can see everything the browser loads as your website loads with the speed tools above, look through them, look at the time and the size of the files and ask yourself if it really needs to be there. If it does can you compress it?

Requests

When someone views your website, it loads up the code and assets from your host web server or CDN to the customers browser. Now if there is content on your website that is not hosted on your web server then it needs to send a request to their servers to pull that information in, to load up the site. The more requests, the larger the external files, the longer it will take to load your website.

Requests can be things like a video hosted on YouTube (your website needs to ask YouTube to send over the information), or a Twitter (your website needs to ask Twitter to send over the information) news feed. Each of these requests will increase the load time. Reducing the speed and user experience.

With requests like YouTube you can just load a thumbnail of the potential video and then **lazy load** the video, when the customer actually clicks on the video. There is no use loading an HD/4K video that may not be watched, which will dramatically slow down your site. Especially if you have ten videos hosted on a page. Using a **light box** plug in linked to a thumbnail can assist here.

Real World Performance And User Experience.

Tests to show how your website speed translates to Google and the devices it is displayed on is one thing but never neglect a real world test. Real world tests can be performed using a ghost or privacy browser. This gives you a real world browsing experience from a new users perspective, without any information being cached or cookies tracking you. If you have friends or family or contacts in the country you need testing ask them to do the same. This way you get real feedback and understand how real people are using your website. Also make sure to a use a variety of browsers, download all the key browsers as more often than not a strange error or resizing issue will be found. Checking your websites on the top browsers will allow you to identify any problems. The top browsers are Chrome, Mozilla Fire Fox, Edge, Safari, Vivaldi, Cake, Opera, Brave, Epic. There are more.

Mobile

Real world tests should be done on mobile as well. In fact mobile first and again use multiple browsers, to test and experience real world results. All the major browsers have a mobile version.

Slowest Website Pages

When testing your website for speed, don't just test you homepage, test your most popular pages. Some slow pages, especially large blogs or products with lots of images etc may have flew under your radar. Make sure every page is optimised for speed, especially key pages that are either getting traffic or you are expecting to get traffic.

Site Security

Website security is so deep it could cover an entire chapter, possibly an entire book. But as this is a layman's guide and we are just covering the basics. The main thing is to make sure your website is safe and secure for customers and then to indicate this to potential customers. Use SSL (Secure Socket Layer) level encryption and move with the times as this evolves into new protocols. This is represented by the green padlock at the top left, next to the websites domain name. The green padlock indicates SSL and a secure website. This is also represented by 'https://' instead of 'http://', the additional **s** is so crucial. Most modern hosting packages will include SSL certification to make your website secure, if they do not offer it for free there may be a small annual fee to implement the protocol. Google most definitely penalises non secure, no https:// websites and moving forward these penalties will become even more severe.

For added reassurance your customers, you can also submit your website for inclusion to Norton, Kaspersky, and other third party vendors that verify the safety of your website. These website also provide badges which can be displayed on your website i.e. verified by Kaspersky. Good for positioning and instilling trust in your audience.

From behind the scenes you can protect your site with a fire wall, and apps like Word Fence and the CDN cloud flare which offer a great level of security for free and paid. Each month detailing what attacks, etc it has defended your website against. Again use this as a positioning in your footer to instil a sense of trust in your potential customers. For example this website is safeguarded by...

Finally, Cloudflare, not only does it hide your who.is data and provide a fast loading website anywhere in the world, it also keeps your website secure.

https://www.cloudflare.com/en-gb/

https://www.wordfence.com

Browser Caching And Compression

Browser caching is essentially allowing the browser to cache or store a little amount of key information from your website to allow regular users of your website to load it faster. e.g. If you use Facebook regularly on the same browser, the website will store key info in your browser so it loads fast, without having to download the entire site each time.

Compression of code reduces the overall weight of a page, and therefore delivers a faster user experience and a faster user experience is key.

GZip is the most common form of data compression in the web apps and website space.

Open Comments Spam

Allowing unregistered comments on your blog is a sure fire way to get spammed. Bots scan through the web looking for blogs and website that have no security or verification features, to their blogs. This allows them to spam, automatically on your blogs comments with links to their respective website , products and services. Google loves backlinks and backlinks from a website with a similar niche are powerful. This is what the bots are doing, they are securing backlinks. So if you run an adventure website, most of the bots should be targeting their spam comments towards similar themed websites. However, we don't want anyone spamming our comments so either turn the comments off (simplest option) or use a plugin to verify the comments making them login via email, or via a link to allow them to use their Google or Facebook account to verify identity. Another way is to use a captcha to verify them.

Captcha

Everyone will have experienced the Captcha verification method at some point while they browse online. The classic, is click all the pictures with a car and you proceed to click them to show that you are not a bot / computer looking to auto spam, the comments, forms etc. There are many kinds of captcha now available, as the bots get more clever the captchas will too. These can be installed on your website at a root level to secure forms, comments etc. Google loves a security focused website.

https://www.google.com/recaptcha/about/

Domain Age

Domain age tells Google that you are a senior and that you have experience, both positives. If your website domain was first registered in 2000 and has been continuously online since, your website has age and has value. Aged domains are often sold for a hearty price.

Domain Renewal

Domain age tells Google that you are serious, buying your domain name for the next ten years, says your in it for the long game. i.e. who.is data says registered in 2021, expires in 2031. This says to Google that this website is serious. It's a low level ranking factor but none the less a ranking factor.

Website Rank Indicators

There are various SEO websites that have done extensive research and have extensive databases into what ranks. From this they can assign a score based on their research and of your website. The most popular is DA which stands for *Domain Authority.* This is a rating for the over all domain. There is also PA which stands for *Page Authority* and this is ranking for the individual pages within the domain. These are the largest and most accurate page and domain indicators outside Google and most websites that either sell old domains or backlinks will refer to domain or pages in terms of DA. Domain Authority which is issued by MOZ. It is out of 100 where higher is better.

Check yours here.
https://Moz.com/domain-analysis
https://Smallseotools.com/domain-authority-checker

Understanding the websites DA, is crucial in analysing backlinks, competitors, keyword research, blog research. This allows you to understand backlinks strength when checking which pages are most popular etc. It allows you to see how powerful a potential backlink is and more.

CMS And Plugins Up To Date

CMS i.e. *content management system* like WordPress, Wix, etc take security extremely seriously. Making sure you have the latest updates, means your website will be patched and ready to fight off almost everything. So make sure that you log in regularly, once a month at least and update the CMS and any plugins you are using to deliver specific functionality within your website. This will make sure that you are best placed to stay safe.

WordPress

I use WordPress to build my websites. There are lots of themes, plugins and additions to add to your WordPress website to make it heavy, slow and sluggish. No matter what you build you will have to start with a clean install of WordPress, then you will add a theme and plug ins on top. Add them sparingly, add only what you need.

I recommend Generate Press. It is a lightweight theme (One of the lightest available, i.e. low page weight) that focuses on speed, stability and accessibility and has a great responsive community. Which is everything you need for a solid foundation to build your website.

https://robb.link/GeneratePress

External Firewall And Website Monitors.

There are many companies that specialise in monitoring and safeguarding your website. This is can be a good option if increased website security is required.

7

Content Is King

You may have heard the idea that content is king. And I preach this non-stop. For me it is the main thing I concentrate on for the various projects I am a part of. Content, is what people are looking for. They are looking for great reviews, how to's, breakdowns, reasons to buy, reasons not to buy. They are looking to understand something that they have no idea about, they are looking for answers. Content that answers the questions people are asking Google, will be shared, will be bookmarked and will be elevated in the eyes of the customer and Google. Good content engages customers, informs customers and closes sales. It is also super important for SEO. The key here is to combine your keyword research into a great piece of content, create something that works for both man and machine.

What To Write About?

Ideas are fairly easy to generate when you think about the purpose your content is serving i.e. to bring customers to your website. With this in mind, simply answer every question you can think of around your product or service.

If I owned a wedding venue I would answer all the questions around the wedding in the area of the venue. Why? When potential customers considering getting married in the area and are looking for photographers, videographers, caterers, DJs, transport, flowers, things to do in the area (guests may be staying local) etc etc, your website, i.e. the venue website, will then keep returning great valuable resources, for a variety of search questions. Each of the articles internally linking to your booking page or availability page.

e.g.

Ten wedding photographers in the Glasgow area.

Ten best wedding bands in the Glasgow area.

Wedding Videographers in the Glasgow area.

Wedding party accommodation in Glasgow.

Then more general questions like.

Why book a wedding venue in Glasgow?

Best Wedding venues in Glasgow?

How much is a wedding venue in Glasgow?

Wedding planners in Glasgow?

Five things every wedding organiser should do.

Five must haves for every wedding

Ten wedding planning mistakes to avoid

Five Scottish wedding traditions stepped in history.

What makes a great wedding?

Five things every wedding needs!

Why a wedding band is better than a wedding DJ

Wedding photos or wedding video or possibly both?

Glasgow Wedding on a budget

Glasgow wedding for under £10K

Glasgow wedding no expense spared!

No matter what your website is about, use your blog to write about and answer all the potential questions your customers will be asking. Bring them to your website indirectly by answering their questions with great value content and always use a 'call to action' and internal linking to direct them to your products and services.

Is The Content Of Value?

With every page on your website you need to ask *is this of value?* If your keyword game or traffic driving skills from social media is on point and you have got people clicking through from Google or social media and they land on a page that is generic and offers now value then they are going to click off. Make sure you're providing great value on every page. I use frase.io to make sure I provide valuable content every time. More info on Fras.io below.

Compelling Messaging

Does each of your pages carry a compelling message, that makes the reader want to share, talks about or buy what ever it is your message is about? It should do. Use the PAS frameworks to create compelling messages. More info on PAS below.

Easily Readable

Not everyone is PHD educated, so using words and sentence structure designed for PHD educated readers may put some visitors off, because they simply do not understand the content. Equally, having lots of quality content that provides value that only you can decipher due to poor written language skills (Grammar, spelling etc) is also a killer. Make sure your content is well written and easily readable.

https://robb.link/ProWritingAid 20% off with code HONEY20

Pro writing aid has many tools to help you write your content. It has over 20 reports and will help you correct your grammar, pacing, structure and more as well as giving your content a Flesch-kincaid reading score. Allowing you to understand the reading level of your content. For more info >> https://prowritingaid.com/art/348/How-to-use...-Readability-Scores.aspx

See the Flesch-kincaid reading score for any page.

https://chrome.google.com/webstore/detail/readability-score/

Helps keep your writing legible, excellent tool.

https://app.grammarly.com

Captivating Headlines

We are not talking click bait here, but we are talking about making your headings (H1 tag) captivating. Make it worthy of being clicked. You want to advertise the value that a potential customers is going to get from visiting your site as well as incorporate your main keyword. Then the key is to deliver with excellent content when they click through to your page. This is the first thing they are going to read, make it good.

Some examples that can be easily interchanged.

Best solutions for...

Best solutions for exploding your BJJ game.

10 best .....

10 best BJJ submissions revealed.

X.. most

Edinburgh's most popular tourist attractions 2022

5 reason why.....

5 reasons why the you need a BJJ training journal.

7 things you need to do before ......

7 things you need to do before starting BJJ classes.

X... explains

The world's best BJJ player explains his top three submission.

X shares...

Elon Musk shares his ideas on first principles thinking.

This is why ....

This is why one good submission is better than ten weak ones.

This is how.....

This is how Brazilian jiu jitsu players are dominating the competition.

The last ..... you'll ever need.

The last BJJ training journal you'll ever need.

You won't believe this.....

You won't believe this BJJ training journal and how it can transform your game.

Why you should stop......

Why you should stop doing Judo and train BJJ.

Relevant Headlines

Head lines need to be relevant. I am not just talking about avoiding clickbait but also keyword stuffing and just being off topic. If your header or title says x then you need to deliver x. It should be as simple as that.

H1, H2, H3, H4, Fonts, Paragraphs

Everyone has read a good blog, set out well and clear. The headers, fonts and paragraph structure all contribute to the quality and value of the blog article or web page. Using a font that is unreadable, too small, too big, not enough contrast etc will make your users experience, a negative one. I like to make the H tags bold so they easily break up the page, I use a clear font with high contrast and make it as easy as possible for the user to navigate through out the page. All of this contributes to the experience and stops the user from bouncing and returning back to Google to check out the competition. Another key factor is using images through out to break up the wall of text.

Spelling

If you have already got a lot of content on you website you can use this tool to find pages with spelling mistakes.

https://typosaur.us

Easy To Scan

When you land on a web page with good content and you start to read but then as soon as you start scrolling the adverts start populating, as the adverts load, the structure of the page changes and as you scroll the paragraphs merge and frustration grows. This is an all too common attempt to make money from ads by providing a poor user experience. Don't, it will not work. Make it as easy as possible for the reader to find their way through your article or page. 300 horrendous pop-ups and ads does not help your user.

Over 650 Words Minimum

As a rule I say over 1000 words, but in reality that can sometimes be difficult, so as a bare minimum 650 words is the lower limit. Google loves good quality and; in depth information as do visitors to your website. Don't be cheap on the words. Tools like Frase.io can help you with this. More info on Frase below.

Quality, Relevant Images

There are many places to get FREE images now a days, sites like https://unsplash.com and https://www.pexels.com, however, try to pick images that are original, preferably shot by you, edited by you etc. If you have a smartphone you can take and edit and original picture. Check out my book Smartphone Smart Marketing for help. Tools like https://robb.link/SEranking have a On page SEO checker which analyses the images on a page and determines if they are unique or not. And if SE Ranking can do it, then Google definitely does it. Images are powerful so don't just regurgitate a common image that is already found all over the internet, give your website original images, just as you give it original written content.

Branded Images

Branded images are a great way to make sure that 1: your images are not stolen by the competition and 2: that no matter where your images go (shares, other sites using them etc) any viewer of the image will be able to find their way back to your site.

Alt Tag Keywords

Alt tags describe an image, they talk to both Google and those with accessibility issues. Describe the image and use your main keywords.

Branded Video

For the same reason we brand images.

Hosted Video On YouTube With The Same Keywords With Links Back To Your Website

YouTube is the second search engine of the internet. And as it is a Google product, it often fares well in search results. As a rule I always encourage a video to be made for each article or page of a website. 1: The YouTube video with the same title will rank before your webpage does, within the content of the video you have your brand and a reference to your product/services and in the description of the video you have a link to the article or page. 2: It is a social signal and soft backlink to your article.

Internally Linking To Key Product Pages

We use internal links to let Google know which is key content or pillar content. Also we use internal lining to link or push potential readers to your product page from your blog etc.

Example - Meditation Journal is the Key page. I write ten different blogs on meditation each with an internal link back to the *meditation journal* page. After all the reason for the blog articles is to get people to buy the Meditation journal. This tells Google that these pages/blogs all support the key page that is the Mediation journal product page.

Call To Action

A call to action is generally at the end of a sales pitch, it is the bit that says. *Book now, buy now, don't miss out on this offer purchase it today.* You have done all this work to get the buyer to your website, use a call to action to encourage them to buy. i.e. After reading this book, please leave a review.

Location Based Content

Google is aware of location, so if you are looking to serve people in a particular locations, use the location in the page or blog title. With the example of the wedding venue above, using the location in the blog content tells Google exactly where the information is targeted at geographically. Another key piece of info for this is to 'geo tag' the photos and embed Google maps for directions on the page. You can also use Schema Mark up to identify location.

Share Buttons

If your content is good make it easy to share. Provide share buttons for the major social media channels. And use a call to action to encourage readers to share. i.e. If you enjoyed this article, please share it with your friends on social media. Click the share button to do so.

No Clickbait

Just don't. Click bait was a big thing a few years ago and it just gets people angry. If you have a title that says "Aliens communicate directly with the Whitehouse in historic first contact" and then people click through to your page that is just full of adverts and no value and with no information about the event because it hasn't happened, people will not come back to your site. The old adage "under promise and over deliver", don't be the online equivalent of the boy who cried wolf.

No Placeholder Text / Lorem Ipsum

If you purchased a website and hit the template button, to build out a generic website with an about page, contact page, blog page etc it may be populated with Lorem Ipsum (i.e. complete gibberish) which is place holder text. e.g.

Lorem ipsum dolor sit amet, consectetur adipiscing elit. Proin hendrerit nec neque sed auctor. Nullam lobortis nisi ac ligula ornare, quis viverra velit lobortis. Fusce dignissim sem vel rhoncus finibus. Phasellus malesuada gravida nisi et consectetur. In faucibus id erat ac pellentesque. Donec non nulla a felis semper euismod vitae ac neque. Mauris aliquam ultrices ultrices. Vivamus tincidunt eu eros sed convallis. Aenean odio turpis, iaculis a porttitor vitae, laoreet a eros.

Nam ornare scelerisque orci quis molestie. Nam magna risus, bibendum ac felis a, iaculis faucibus diam. Fusce imperdiet, ipsum at efficitur pretium, velit quam lobortis est, vitae ultrices nibh orci sit amet ligula. Suspendisse condimentum augue quis magna elementum, in porta justo consequat. Praesent sagittis suscipit felis, aliquet placerat nisi lacinia in. Duis a dignissim eros, at dictum lectus. Fusce at faucibus leo. In nec mi lectus. Praesent finibus turpis efficitur metus mollis rutrum. Nunc a nisl congue, rhoncus metus nec, hendrerit est.

Be sure to check all your pages, if your customer enjoyed an article and checks out your about page or contact page and it's full of gibberish i.e. Lorem Ipsum, then they may not return. It indicates that your website is not even complete. It demonstrates a lack of attention to detail and effort and that says a lot about your attitude towards customer services etc.

PAS Framework (Problem- Agitate- Solution.)

P.A.S is a great frame work for product pages. Often, marketers are so focused on the product and its features, they neglect the emotional connection that needs to be established with the target audience.

PAS framework is a proven way to keep your copywriting focused on why the product is important.

Problem: Present the problem, define what is wrong.

Agitate: Get specific, get into the granular details and reasons of the problem. Touch on the emotions.

Solution. Offer your solution. Call to action.

Why I Use Frase.io For Writing SEO Optimised Page And Blog Content?

Frase.io is a game changing tool for writing SEO optimised content for your website, perfect for product pages or blogs.

Frase.io allows you to type in a question, statement, or heading i.e. a long tail keyword that you want to optimise for. It then scans the top results from Google around that question or keyword, averages out all the information and tells you all the key information that you need to include to have a chance of ranking. Yes, it does most of the work for you!

For me, the key tool here is seeing what sort of topics are being covered for the particular question or keyword. Frase.io shows you which topics are being covered and how many times that topic or keyword is being referenced on average in the content and in the headers. So at a glance I can see what I need to write about to cover all the bases of the most successful articles/pages competing for that keyword. It has a handy word document with auto save, so everything can be done right there. As you write your content, blog or article, Frase.io highlights the topics your article has covered and shows you clearly all the topics/keywords/headers that you still need to cover, giving you a topic score to keep you on track. For instance I typed in "Understanding Meditation" as a start. Frase.io tells me that the average content for the first page of SERP websites is

Words: 2149, Headers: 5, Images: 2, Domain Authority: 88, Backlinks: 4584

Which tells me that this is a hard topic to rank for directly. The article has to have depth, be well researched and worthy of being shared. A DA of 88 is high! and 2148 words is meaty. This chapter is around 3000 words, which gives you an idea of the kind of length that is required. Now when I go and write my article in Frase.io I click on the topic scores and see all the keywords or topics that are currently being covered by the first page results on Google and if I want any chance of replacing one of the competition, I must at least cover all these topics at a minimum to provide a similar level of value that is already being provided by the competition.

Here are some of the topics Frase highlighted I must cover for an article on "Understanding Meditation" to be competitive.

"Mindfulness-Based Stress Reduction, effects of meditation, blood pressure, transcendental meditation, health benefits, mindfulness-based cognitive therapy, quality of life, irritable bowel syndrome, physical health, breath work"

As you write in Frase you can also select to show all the keywords that you are missing, i.e the gaps that you must cover to be competitive. Another fantastic feature in Frase is the Content Brief, it will generate you a content outline, instantly. Covering keywords (short, long, clusters), headers, questions, stats and more which gives you a really great place to start a new article from. Combine Frase with independent keyword research, insider knowledge of a topic and great on page SEO (headers, images, fast loading page etc) and you are sure to be competitive, no matter the topic.

Note: You can achieve everything Frase does manually, it just takes more time and a spread sheet.

https://robb.link/Frase

Ideas Bonus

https://alltop.com is a fantastic place to see the headline of hundreds of top performing pages in your niche. See what's hot and beat it.

8

TECHNICAL SEO OVERVIEW

Technical SEO is super important. Great content that provides value is one thing, but if your technical SEO is no good, you will not rank!! Technical SEO is about helping Google search bots or "Spiders" to find, crawl and index your website.

For my website, which I run on Wordpress I use Rank Math to assist me with some of these items, however another popular plugin is Yoast. For other CMS you will need to Google for options.

https://rankmath.com

https://yoast.com

SEO Audit

Sites like https://robb.link/SERPstat, https://robb.link/SEranking, https://www.seotesteronline.com, https://www.seoptimer.com, https://website.grader.com, https://www.seobility.net/and more will provide you with a site wide audit. Highlighting lots of the topics addressed in this chapter. My website scores 95/100 on some and 58/100 on others, showing there is not standard thought in the dark art of SEO. These audits are a great place to start and must have tool, to track your progress over time.

Let Google Know You Are Here

So there are a number of things you can do to let Google know that you are trying. These items are not about great content and value, these items are about letting Google know you understand web technologies and are doing your best to inform them that your web site is conforming. In this section we look at the basics of what a standard website should be doing.

Accessible To Search Engines

Making your website accessible to Google is fairly simple. Following the standard rules of web design will almost guarantee that your website will be indexed by Google and the other big players over time. However, this can take time. To speed up the process and make sure that Google knows that you are there, you can register to Google analytics and Google Search Console. If you have a physical location create a Google My Business account to assist in letting Google know that you exist and are ready to play ball.

Google Search Console.

Search console provides some key data, and allows you to see information not accessible in Google analytics. However, you can integrate your Google Search Console account into your Google Analytics account to get the majority of the information in one platform. Here in GSC you can authenticate your website ownership and upload your sitemap.xml file. You can also run a Coverage Report which lets you see if your website is being fully indexed by Google. Once set up you can integrate your search console account and data into most SEO software like SERanking and SerpStat and more. Allowing them direct data from your website.

Google Analytics

Linking your website to Google Analytics is essential to understanding how your website is fairing. This tool allows you to see lots of quality data about your audience, click through rate, which devices folk are using, which countries, sales, conversions, traffic sources and more. So making sure that you have an account set up and your website is linked is crucial. This is an easy enough process and Google has examples and walk throughs on its site.

Sitemap.xml File

The site map is super important! The site map is a document that shows all the pages and structure of your website. It's one of the ways the search bots understand a page and the main way that Google bots find new URLs. In SEO, if there is a tool that will make Google's job easier then we do it. Site maps are one of these things. Most websites will have a setting for automatic generation of a site map. Head over to Search Console and click on Sitemaps to see how Google sees your sitemap. If it doesn't you can add the URL of your sitemap. If your website doesn't have this function then check out these websites.

www.xml-sitemaps.com

https://rankmath.com Free SEO plugin for WordPress websites generates site maps.

Check any website's site map with SEO Meta one click > Summary Tab > just under half way down on the right hand side.

The purpose of the sitemap is to show Google all the pages on your website that are working, so check over your pages with the **SEO Minion** chrome extension to make sure all your internal links are working.

Schema Mark-Up

Schema markup is another tool that tells Google exactly what the page of the website is for, this uses microdata. For example the schema markup for a page could tell Google that the page contains a recipe, a book, a local business, or a product. This code tells Google the ins and outs of the page and is one of the keys to getting your web page into Googles SERP Features and onto voice search. "SERP Features" are the Google generated info boxes that now appear at the top of SERPS. Recipe cards, maps, products etc.

Learn more about schema markup

https://schema.org

https://support.google.com/webmasters/answer/3069489?hl=en

Generate your schema markup

https://technicalseo.com/tools/schema-markup-generator/

https://rankmath.com Free SEO plugin for WordPress websites generates schema mark-up.

Check any pages Schema Markup.

SEO Meta one click, go to the website > click on SEO meta > then the Social tab > scroll down past FB and twitter.

SEO Meta one click, go to the website > click on SEO meta > then the tools tab > then click microdata, microformats and RDFa

Sufficient Page Content

Google loves content, and so do web users. They love clear, coherent content. Do not short change someone that ends up on your website with 35 words. Bring the depth and details. As a general rule of thumb I try for a minimum of 650 words per page or per blog, with some blogs reaching into the thousands. Blogs that have depth and detail are the most likely chance of being saved, bookmarked and shared. When something has value it will generate traffic and positive SEO. Even on pages with little information make sure there is content for good on page SEO.

Duplicate Content

Content that is identical or very similar will be considered duplicate content by Google. The questions is how does Google prioritise these similar pages? First thing is you should not have pages with Identical content. There is no need, but if you do, you need to tell Google which is the preferred URL and this is called Canonicalization. Imagine a road sign that says supermarket first left and opposite it across the road there is another sign for the same supermarket that says supermarket first right. Yes, it would be confusing, duplicate content confuses Google, it doesn't know which to rank and cause keyword cannibalization. Duplicate Titles and H1 headings can work the same way.

You can add to your Robots.txt file to indicate a particular page should not be indexed.

Find duplicate content with a website audit. Both SEranking and SerpStat as well as many others offer this.

If you have a few pages that are duplicate and they are both ranking you can determine which page is better by checking Google Search Console, checking your SEO software of choice to see which page is ranking better for keywords, which page is driving more traffic, etc. Once you have decided which page to keep, you can set a 301 redirect from the duplicate pages URL (the one being deleted) to the main content URL (the one being kept). This means that even though the page has been removed it will be redirected to the content.

Canonical URLs

Canonical URLs are great for web pages that have similar content where the above methods are not needed. i.e On an eCommerce website where a variation in colour or size generates a very similar page. You can use the Canonical tag on the main version of the item to say that this is the main one, the main content. More about canonical tags here>>

https://developers.google.com/search/docs/advanced/crawling/consolidate-duplicate-urls

Site Structure

A website can be a beautifully organised bastion of information that was conceived and built from the ground up or it can be a higgelty piggelty maze of madness. By creating a coherent, well thought out site structure you make both Google and your human visitors life's easier. A strong, efficient structure makes every other aspect of SEO easier.

I use https://www.seotesteronline.com to allow me to see the site structure of my website and competitors websites. However, a great free site for visualising the structure is http://www.visualsitemapper.com

Example I use /books/..... for my books and /news/.... for my blogs. I doesn't have to be overly complicated just clear.

https://www.robbwallace.co.uk/**books**/smartphone-smart-marketing/

https://www.robbwallace.co.uk/**books**/80-plus-ideas-to-market-your-business/

https://www.robbwallace.co.uk/**news**/5-marketing-strategies-for-authors/

https://www.robbwallace.co.uk/**news**/best-software-for-indie-authors/

Breadcrumbs

Just like the idea from the fairly tale, the bread crumbs allow you see where you are on the website and easily navigate back the way.

Page Speed.

Make sure that each page is fast, not just the homepage. Each page needs to be fast.

Check any page for speed with SEO Meta one click > Tools Tab > GT Metrix

Or read over the Speed chapter for alternative websites and tools.

Human.txt

Is a fairly new thing. But all the major players now have them from Google, Netflix etc. It tells Google about the people behind the website. Read more here > https://humanstxt.org

http://www.google.com/humans.txt

http://www.nytimes.com/humans.txt

http://www.netflix.com/humans.txt

http://www.adultswim.com/humans.txt

Responsive Mobile First Website

Make your website accessible via mobile. Use a responsive theme.

Meta Title & Descriptions

These are the items that show up in the SERP i.e. in the Google search result. The Meta description and title should contain your keyword as well as a call to action. Meta description length is a key SEO factor that will come up in almost every SEO software running a scan of your page. What comes up in the SERP is determined by your meta description. Google SERPs only show 160 characters worth of information. So learning to say what you need to say in a short space whilst including your keywords is a dark art. This could be the only opportunity you get to hook a potential visitor. This is the first thing they see on Google's results page about your website. Make sure it is better than the competitions! Look at what you competition are saying and make yours better. Be direct, offer a solution and include your keywords. You have 160 characters to do this.

Check any page title and description with SEO Meta one click > Summary Tab.

WWW Resolve

Google sees the domains four ways. www.robbwallace.co.uk, robbwallace.co.uk, https://robbwallace.co.uk https://www.robbwallace.co.uk

Each of these being a separate website, resolving the website just means that no matter what address is typed in it resolves to the correct one set by you, allowing Google to see you as one domain property. Also stops Google seeing duplicates of your website. i.e. https://robbwallace.co.uk is what I have set. If you type in any of the other three options it will resolve to the former automatically.

Https

Make sure your using HTTPS and that your website is secure.

https://letsencrypt.org

Identify And Fix Broken Links

Install SEO minion, go to the webpage you need to check and click SEO minion, then click Check Broken Links. It will then run through every link on the page and show you which links are broken if any. If you find any, fix them. i.e. correct the address, most of the time it is a simple spelling mistake, other times an internal page or external page may no longer exist. If this is the case update the link.

https://chrome.google.com/webstore/detail/seo-minion/giihipjfimkajhlcilipnjeohabimjhi

Alt tags

Alt tags on an image are for accessibility. The alt tag tells Google as well as partially sighted individuals what the image is. i.e. A horse, a black t shirt, a woman with a coffee cup. In SEO we tend to use it to describe the image and add in a keyword or two.

Check any web pages image alt tags with SEO Meta one click > Image Tab.

Open Graph

When you paste your URL into a social media platform, being Twitter or Facebook, the social media platform will pull through an image from the website. If you do not designate the image it will pull through the main image attached to your page or home page. Designating an image is the best practice. If your site is large and you blog regularly, then you should be designating the images to make sure that the correct image gets pulled through and thus the social media post displays the appropriate imagery for the shared URL. If you share a page on trainers and the image on social shows up as trousers, you are making it easier for your customers to click away and search out other options.

Check any pages Open Graph

SEO Meta one click > go to the website > click on SEO meta > then the Social tab.

SEO Meta one click > go to the website > click on SEO meta > then the tools tab > then click on Check Open Graph properties or scroll further and click on Twitter card validator.

Backlinks

There is an entire chapter dedicated to the Backlinks. As noted earlier, we believe there are over 200 ranking factors, and within the various schools of thought on SEO, backlinks are universally regarded as a key ranking factor. A backlink is essentially a digital word of mouth. Having a website in a similar niche or a website with authority give a link to your website tells Google that this article or page is worthy of reading or being indexed. Backlinks are hard to come by, but we will get you started.

9

BACKLINKS

As mentioned earlier, backlinks are the Gold in SEO. Having a solid backlink strategy and making sure that you dedicate time to the darkest of arts is the way to make serious gains.

The Domain Authority of a given website is a key factor in the strength of the backlink and of the potential juice that will be transferred from the domain via a backlink. As a rule, if the website is a large institute, news provider, university, government, or brand then the weight or juice generated from a backlink will be worth the sweat and tears it took to get it.

The other key thing to look for in backlinks is niche ore relevance. We want to secure backlinks from the same niche because this tells Google that your peers are saying that you are one of them and that they associate you as one of them. i.e. A fishing blog, linking to your fishing products. Or a camping blog linking to your camping 101 article. This is true digital word of mouth and a form of digital thumbs up.

Analyse Competitors Link Profile

The quickest and most efficient way to find relevant websites that are linking to websites similar to yours is by checking out your competitions backlink profile. This just means, who is linking to them? i.e. what backlinks have they secured? By doing this you can see the websites that are linking in and potentially reach out to them in a similar fashion. If you do your research and you see that they have a number of local directories, magazines, discussion platforms and forums, then you can go to these pages and try to get yourself a similar backlink. We call this outreach.

When researching the competitor's backlink profile make a note of the kind of content that is attracting the backlinks. Is the content a best selling product, a product review, long blog, info graphic, interview, how tos, free items, cheap items, offers etc etc.

Understand if there are any common themes to the content that is getting backlinks, is it covering popular content and trends? Make notes on the kind of word count, keywords, headers, language, images etc that they are using on these pages that are receiving backlinks. Finally make a note of the highest DA (Domain Authority) sites and target these first, if applicable.

Outreach And Brand Building

We can divide backlinks into two main categories. Outreach and Brand building. Outreach can be further broken down into niche links.

Brand Building, Citations, Link Directories.

These are spaces online where you create an account, fill in your details and offer your services, post relevant details etc.

This can be everything from social media channels, to podcasts, to local business directories. There are literally tens of thousands of these pages out there. So take a day, arm yourself with a large pot of coffee, a spread sheet and get hammering away. There is a good list to get you started in chapter 25.

Outreach

Simply reaching out to the thousands of articles and discussions related to your industry, product or service. This can be Quora, Facebook groups, online forums, blogs, news sites, magazines, colleges, universities and more. As the name suggests this is active work. Create a spreadsheet and work your way through.

For discussion sites like Quora you just need to set up an account and start answering questions but as a rule only backlink to your website or specific webpage with one in three answers. Anything more will get you flagged and seen as a spammer. And always bring value and quality with your answers. Quora's answers get upvoted so the best answers naturally rise to the top and have the most click through traffic.

Just sign up to forums and be active. Start slow and participate, show your worth and over time share a few links.

Contact local news, general magazines, radio etc and let them know you exist, see if they will run an article and always ask for that backlink.

Contact Universities, colleges and schools, tell them you are a graduate and ask if they can cover your current project in their graduates newsletter or on the main website.

The main way I build links for my job (yes, I work part time) is through niche magazines and blogs. But once you leave a positive review and buy a further twenty copies of this book for all your colleagues I may be able to write full time! Anyway, I work for a large sporting goods company. I send out products to niche magazines and bloggers for review and make sure that they know that I need an article written and a backlink generated. This way I am getting my employer eyeballs on the product via their blog or magazines audience, as well as gaining a niche backlink. Don't pay for the review just send the product. Money well spent.

Niche Links

Method 1:

Search for Magazines and blogs in your niche.

Find the article and find the contact and either suggest to them that the article can be improved by adding in A,B,C or that you would be willing to write a similar article as you are an expert in A,B,C.

Always make sure the site is a good fit for your content, do your research to make sure of this and then get in touch.

Hello [Name],

How are you? Your recent article on [one of their popular articles relevant to your niche] was excellent, I really enjoyed it. Very informative. I would love to contribute an article on [Your Niche] for my website [Your Website]. I have some topic ideas that I think your audience will enjoy:

Idea #1, Idea #2, Idea #3, Idea #4, Idea #5

Do you think your readers would be interested in any of these topics? I can work to any deadline and wordcount you require. I will also push out any articles generated from this collaboration across my social media and newsletter network.

Thank you,

[Your Name]

When they reply, write them a quality piece, worthy of their magazine/website and send it over, stating which page on your website to link to. Once it is published make sure the link is generated, if not follow up to make sure it is. Thank them and tell them to get in touch if they need more articles in the A,B,C fields that you specialise in.

Method 2:

Finding every magazine, website, social media influencer with a blog and YouTube channel.

If you have a physical product, ask them to review it. Send them a free or loan copy. They get something awesome to generate great new content for their channel and you get a review. Great for any kind of ecommerce brand. Just makes sure you make it clear that you need a backlink generated from their website or blog, and YouTube links in the descriptions of videos are powerful too.

Method 3:

Securing Backlinks with great content.

Make sure your content is worthy of being linked to, so that when other folk in your niche write about aspects about your industry they reference your articles as places for further reading, or the product to have etc etc.

Method 4:

Take an article that you have written for someone and take to social media to offer a free article or blog written for them in exchange for a backlink. A great place for this is Facebook groups. There will be a lot of website owners too busy to generate content, ready to bite your hands off for free content.

Method 5:

Steal competitors broken backlinks

Once you have found popular articles that link to your competitors, scan them with SEO Minion to determine if any of the links in these articles are broken or just manually open them all up in new tabs. i.e. they go to a website that is no longer there, these links are 404s. Whatever that link was i.e. check out Johnson.com's list of top ten marketing books and when you click the link in the article goes to a 404 on the webpage, i.e. a 404 on your competitors website. You can capitalise on this. First you need to replicate that content or you may have already generated a similar article. Any case, once that is done you now need to contact the website to inform them that the x and xs link is broken and providing a poor experience for their readers. Offer up your article and link to solve the issue.

Hello [Editors name or generic magazine website name.],

My name is [YOUR NAME], and I am the [INSERT JOB ROLE – i.e., MARKETING, SEO manager] at [COMPANY'S NAME or WEBSITE].

I was reading [INSERT THEIR POST TITLE], great article. Very informative. However, when I clicked on the [INSERT LINK] on that post, it directed me to a 404 page, i.e the link is broken. Not good. I was going to head back to Google then I thought I can help these guys. You are probably aware that 404s are bad for user experience, which is the reason for my email. I recently published an in-depth article on the same subject as the broken link in your article:

[INSERT YOUR POST TITLE].

Here's the link to our article: [URL].

Check it out, I think your readers would love it. Please feel free to link to our article instead of the 404 page you are currently linking to, as our article will provide your audience with a live website and a better user experience. We update this article regularly to make sure our patrons get the best and most current information.

Thanks you, I look forward to hearing from you. Any questions, let me know.

[YOUR NAME]

This is not going to get a back link every time, more like one in ten but that is the backlink game.

Method 6: Email

I received this email at work - I have changed some details (I am not advertising them) however, the idea is pretty sound and can be replicated by anyone. It plays on the fear of missing out (FOMOI), lack of SEO knowledge, a badge (positioning/trust) and a deadline. These guys have built a massive backlink footprint using this technique.

Hi,

I hope you're well.

It's Jane from xxxxxxx - our Best Bike Phone Holder article is now live, and you can see who made the final cut here:

INSERT web url reviewing multiple products. *(*Their's was a blog review with many bike phone mounts. **Our's was no on the list! (FOMO**)

Unfortunately, as we didn't hear back from you, we have not included your Bike Handle Bar Mount .

The good news is that it's still not too late to get Bike Handle Bar Mount listed with a direct link to your sales page. **(Promising a backlink)**

Just reply to this email with confirmation that you're happy for us to include your product, and answer the question: 'what makes your product stand out?' We'll then get your Bike Handle Bar Mount included and give you our ***best of Bike Phone Holder badge that you can use on your website*** *to showcase to potential customers.* **(Everyone loves a badge)**

Our 15 Best Free Yoga Apps and 13 Best Weighted Hula Hoop articles bring in 6000+ visitors each month, and rank within the top 3 positions on Google. As you can see, this kind of content is a hit with our readers - and we expect this article to be just as successful: **(Promising Gold)**

It will be sent out to our 2.3m subscriber base tomorrow, who are all within your target demographic. If you want to get the Bike Handle Bar Mount in front of them too, get back to me by close of business today and I'll ensure it's included :)

All the best,

Jane

When I replied to Jane, asking what next, she asked me to add the article link to our products sales page. Showing our customers her blog article. A backlink for a backlink. There is a lot of ideas to be mined from this email. Best of luck.

Method 7

Monitor your brand, this can be done via software like https://sociality.io or by searching for your brand in Google "Robb Wallace" using quotation marks. Once you find websites mentioning you without backlinks you can contact them and ask for them to add the link. They have already mentioned you, which makes these, potentially some of the easiest backlinks to get.

Method 8

When researching your competitors, you may come across pages with backlinks that are extremely poor. The content is poor, low word count, poor understanding of the subject matter, slow load times etc. Contact each of the websites that are linking to the article and provide them with your article. Your article, by comparison will be better in every respect and therefore better for them and their customers.

Method 9

If you are an industry expert or trusted voice in the niche, lend your name and brand to reviews or testimonials on websites. This way the website or article gets a bonified endorsement by an industry leader and you get a backlink to your website.

Leverage PR

There are many free and paid PR services. These are great for getting into Google news feeds and getting your product or service featured in large news outlets. These PR services range from Free (Limited) to $1000s. Select one appropriate for your budget and upload your press release, images, videos and links and hit enter. These can be great for an instant SEO boost, especially if the PR company/individual knows what they are doing.

These guys have a good reputation.
https://legiit.com/SpinePR/

Skyscraper Technique

This is all about great content that is worthy of being shared.

1: Research to find the most shared articles in your niche. Websites like https://contentstudio.io, https://buzzsumo.com show articles with the most shares. You can also use websites like http://socialsignalscheck.com to check how many social signals an article has. Combine this information with a backlink check of the article.

2: Once you have determined what is the most popular content in your niche, note down which websites shared that content.

3: Write a better piece of content, make it better in everyway. More concise, better information, easier to read, easier to understand, easier to implement, more depth, better examples etc.

4: Contact all the website and social media platforms, influencers etc that shared the original article informing them and encouraging them to share yours with their audience. State the benefits.

This will require a lot of coffee, but rising to the top is not for everyone!

Referring Domains

You really want to secure domains with the highest amount of domain authority. Those with a DA of 50 and above will really get the needle moving.

Most SEO software will have a basic backlink feature. This will at a minimum show you the referring domains, ie the domains that link to your website.

Websites For Social Shares On Articles

Paid

https://buzzsumo.com

https://contentstudio.io

http://socialsignalscheck.com

Backlink Checkers Free

https://smallseotools.com/backlink-checker/

https://ahrefs.com/backlink-checker

https://monitorbacklinks.com/seo-tools/backlink-checker

https://www.seoreviewtools.com/valuable-backlinks-checker/

Paid

https://robb.link/SERPstat

https://robb.link/SEranking

10

NEW SEARCH

Search is ever evolving, today there are multiple ways to search and in the future there will be even more ways to ask the machines. Here, we will look at a few of the ways in which we can attempt to get ahead of the competition.

Main Keywords Voice Search

Voice search is a great tool that is becoming more and more popular due to the accessibility it brings in key situations. For example driving, when your hands are occupied and of course home devices like Google home, Siri and Amazon Alexa. The main competitors in voice search are Apple's Siri, Google Assistant, Amazon's Alexa and Microsoft Cortana. Take your main keywords and main questions that you are ranking for or expecting to rank for and speak them into your devices. The interesting thing about voice search is it is even more brutal than standard Google searches because most of the time it only returns one answer. So if your SEO sucks, you are not going to be showing up on voice search any time soon.

Voice Vs Type

With traditional type based search we have become so adept at it that we now more than ever, cut straight to the chase. We type "Restaurants Glasgow" and allow Google to doe its magic. But when we speak into a voice assistant, we are more likely to say something like "Google, I am looking for good restaurants in the Glasgow area". The way we use voice to search is fundamentally long tail keywords and more question based.

How Do You Rank On Voice Search?

1: Conversational long tail keywords are more in line with voice search than shorter, straight to the point keyword searching. If targeting voice search, make your article headers long tail and more speech like.

2: Create lots of FAQ style pages and content. These pages are designed to answer simple questions concisely, this is what voice is really good at delivering just now.

i.e Strong H2's that are questions, followed by either short paragraphs or short lists.

3: Use Schema Mark up to clarify to Google what the article is about. And start securing SERP Features and featured snippets

SEM Rush 2020 voice research study showed 60% of of answers returned from voice search occupied a SERP feature!

https://www.semrush.com/blog/voice-search-local-seo/

Implementing SEO For Web Articles For Web And Voice

1: Generate a question to use as your title H1

2: Answer that question in a short concise manner at the top of your page.

3: Use the rest of the article to cater for traditional search SEO

4: Add Schema Markup to let Google know exactly what the article is about.

Main Keywords Image Search

Another popular search to dominate is the image search. We do this by making sure we name our images appropriately and use ALT tags. This way Google knows what the image is and indexes it. If you name your images xyz or abc1 then it's going to show up in image searches for abc etc. If your website is about marketing books, then name your images marketing-book.jpg which has more chance of being indexed and showing up when someone searches for this term in Googles image search.

Google Image Search

Head on over to https://images.google.com and upload your image to search via images. This at the moment allows you to see what websites are using similar images and then allows you to see how they are labelling and naming those images. At some point in the future, Google will understand all images embedded in a website. Just now we need to inform it with a name and label.

Main Keywords Video Search

Video search is big business and ranking well on YouTube is powerful. As more and more people look for videos to fix something, understand something, watch a review etc. The more these videos will appear on both standard and voice search. I always try to make a video with a similar headline for every article or webpage I create. Why? As the YouTube video always gets indexed and ranked before my page and therefore has more chance of turning up fast on voice search.

Main Keywords Return Google Snippets.

Google snippets are an ever evolving beast. And as noted above are one of the keys to voice search. I am convinced that the future of Google, is to index and display the web on the SERP page via SERP Features. I.e. No need for the customer to actually go to your website. The correct information is extracted and displayed right there in the search results. This is already happening to a degree just now with Googles SERP features and featured snippets. If you search for a recipe, weather, currency conversion, opening times, cinema times, sport results and more you will find that Google displays the most relevant answer in a featured snippet right there on the search results. This is good and it's bad, it is good that your result is so good it gets featured as a snippet and bad because the information served was so good, i.e. Google extracted the correct content from your website that the customer doesn't need to go to your website. Circumnavigating your website completely. Is this the future of Google? We will have to wait and see. For now getting a featured snippet can be a good thing as it lists your site at the top of search and it may be enough to get them to click through and book mark your page.

SERP Features To Win.

Most of these are secured by using schema markup and micro data, to inform Google what your page is about. This is just a few there are many more and more added all the time.

Featured Snippet

Google uses information from a single website to answer the questions asked. This answer is highlighted at the top of the SERP results.

Local Pack

Or map pack shows three results on a map listing for local or geographically orientated searches. Type in "Curry near me"

Reviews

Shows the reviews generated for a product or service in the SERP. Type in "Smartphone Smart Marketing Robb Wallace" and on my listing you will see the reviews, generated by Schema mark-up.

Related Questions/People Also Ask

Questions are generated related to the question you ask. Type in "Facts about space"

Sitelinks

If you search for a specific brand or domain, Google may display links under the SERP to other key pages of the website. Type in "unique adventure tours Scotland"

Image Pack

A selection of images displayed horizontally across the top of SERPS. Type in "Images of a dog"

Knowledge Graph

Generates a panel of information about people, companies, authors, sports etc.. Type in "Smartphone Smart Marketing Robb Wallace"

Knowledge Card

This usually displays data. Try it by typing in "Population of Scotland"

Top Ads, Bottom Ads

Google ads served at the Top and bottom of SERP results. Join Google ads.

Shopping Results

Another form of Google ads.

Twitter

Displays relevant tweets at the top of SERPs. Type in "Biden on twitter"

11

Legal

These items are generally relegated to the footer of the website and most small websites overlook these items. But in the grand scheme of things SEO, they contribute to the trust and authentication signals you are sending both Google and your customers. These also contribute to customer experience, being able to read the privacy policy or returns information is crucial if selling products or services on your website.

GDPR Popup

The General Data Protection Regulation (GDPR) is a regulation in Europe that came into effect on May 25, 2018. Make sure, if you are capturing data from clients in the EU that you have a GDPR popup to notify them.

Cookie Policy

Cookies are small text files that are stored on your device when you visit certain websites. They are used to track user activity on websites and can be used for marketing purposes. The cookie settings on most websites are set to "allow cookies" to give customers the best browsing experience possible. Or should that be give us the best tracking experience possible. Always give the customer the option to decide which level of cookie is being applied to them.

Privacy Policy

A privacy policy is a statement that describes how your personal information will be used and shared when you use a website. If you're taking any form of customer details be sure to have a privacy policy that is accessible.

Terms & Conditions

Terms and conditions are the terms and conditions that govern the customer's use of your website. These include any rules, regulations, policies, guidelines, or laws that apply to them when using this website.

Returns Policy

The returns policy states the time frame and conditions in which a customer can replace the item after purchase.

Clear Customer Services Contact

A clear contact for customer services, hiding your customer phone number and contact is a sure fire way to lose trust and make sure the customer will not return for repeat business.

Website Copyright In Footer

Add the year and copyright. Basic, simple and adds to the authentication of the site.

Charity No

If you are a charity or similar organisation display your number for easy access and authentication.

FAQ (Frequently Asked Questions)

A FAQ can be used to cover all these points around privacy, returns, customer services etc.

12

ACCESSIBILITY

Not every web user is the same or has the same capacity to access your website and the information held within it. Making your website as accessible as possible 1: Ticks off boxes that Google loves to see and 2: Makes your products and services available to even more potential customers.

> "Despite this, the study found that 71% of individuals with disabilities will abandon a website that's difficult to use. This results in an estimated loss of £11.75 billion (or approximately $14.4 billion) each year in the United Kingdom alone." www.forbes.com/sites/ryanrobinson/2019/09/25/website-accessibility-online-business

Full ADA/WCAG 2.1 Compliance

Full compliance means that all web pages have been reviewed for accessibility issues and are fully accessible to people using assistive technology.

ALT Text For Images

ALT text for images is an alternative way to describe the image content in the HTML document. This can be used when the image cannot be displayed due to some technical reason. Or give more description to someone who is partially sighted.

Captions / Transcripts For Audio & Video

Captions/Transcripts for audio and video files are text descriptions that appear on top of the media file. They can be used to describe what is happening in the video or audio clip. Captions are often used when listening to music or watching movies.

Text Size & Readability Adjustments

Allows your customers to change the readability of the text by changing font size, line spacing, font colour and background colour.

Colour Contrast Adjustments

Colour contrast adjustments for accessibility reading means that the colour contrast between text and background is increased so that people who have low vision can read the content on screen.

Descriptive Link Text

Descriptive link text is the text that appears in the link itself. This can be used to describe what the link does, or to provide additional information about the link. For example, if you have a link to an article on Wikipedia, you might use descriptive link text like "Wikipedia Article" or "Learn more about this topic."

Navigation & Site Structure

Navigation & Site Structure accessibility refers to the ability of people with disabilities to access and use information and communication technology (ICT) for daily life activities. This includes the physical environment, equipment, software, and services that enable ICT use. I.e. making sure that someone using a special pointer or who is colour deficient or has no hearing is still able to access every aspect of the site.

Audits

audit.deque.com

https://www.webaccessibility.com

www.accessibilitychecker.org

Tools

https://userway.org/compare/

13

MESSENGER/CHAT

Chat is the next big thing. In China it is already the current big thing, everything is done within the wee chat app. Dentist appointment, hailing a cab, buying food from a market vender, commenting and interacting with the web and social. WhatsApp, Facebook messenger, Telegram etc are all becoming more popular for answering customer requests and queries. As they do increase their functionality, more and more users will use them for answering basic search like queries.

The other major benefit of chat apps is the quick response customers get to their query, which increase the customer experience and leads to more positive customer experiences and reviews. Are you making it easy for your customers to contact/ purchase via chat?

Facebook Messenger

Facebooks messenger app has some advantages if you do a lot of your social media via Facebook. You can set automated responses to key questions and you can if you chose install the app on your phone and have yourself or a staff members answer the questions as they come in. When installing messenger use a click to open function. Do not install the Facebook plugin or code direct from Facebook. This will increase your website's request, page size and load time. Click to open works just fine. i.e. the potential customer clicks on the link or Facebook messenger icon and it opens the app on their phone or desktop. No need for it to generate a chat environment on your website.

What's App Business

If WhatsApp is your social flavour add a link to it.

Messenger Comment And Receive

If using messenger on your website, make sure you respond to the customers who use it. It does not have to be instant but a response has to be made. Otherwise it is just another avenue to provide a poor user experience and bad SEO.

14

Social Media

Which channels are you using?

Every year new social media channels appear and every year old social media channels fall from grace. Friendster, Bebo, Myspace, AOL messenger were all huge when I grew up. Now it is Facebook, Instagram, TikTok etc that the mass majority of folks use.

Google's analytics show where the traffic to your website originates, be it organic, direct, social media etc, and some websites generate a big percentage of their traffic from social. These are great platforms for distributing your website's content. There are many all round social media platforms like Facebook that offer a bit of everything for everyone and there are specific platforms like LinkedIn and Pinterest. The key to social media is choosing the platforms that 1: you enjoy using 2: that your potential audience enjoy using. This way you will continue to update the platform with content as you build and engage your audience. Opening an account for every platform is good to register it, and to grab your specific handle i.e "@robbauthor" but maintain at least one channel that you actively participate in. One channel to rule them all, one that you inform the audience of the others that you are most active on.

Each platform needs content tweaked for it, be it character length, video length, word limits, hyper link urls etc.

Things to do for all platforms.

1: Secure the same handle if possible i.e @robbauthor Don't have @robbauthor, @authorrobb, @robb1234 @Authorof SSM - Be consistent in your branding.

2: Fill in and populate each platform with your brand image, URL, and description.

3: Use familiar keywords and categories to allow searchers of the native search feature of each platform to locate your posts.

4: Jump on any new feature as soon as it is released, e it Live, Stories, etc etc. When a platform pushes a new feature they increase the reach it gets to entice the community to use it. Take advantage of the extended reach and get your message out there.

4: Research competitor's content and replicate anything that is driving engagement.

Facebook

Facebook has lots of features and facilities.

Advantages - URL from Facebook to external websites are permitted.

Facebook groups are one of the best sources for website traffic. Either start your own group or join one or two related to your business product or theme. This is the best way to get external links to your website from Facebook. Some Facebook groups can see hundreds of posts a day and active groups like this will have a legion of dedicated users. Integrating and influencing them will require work. Establish yourself as a regular contributor, make friends with the admins, respond to user questions with authority and offer up your blog posts for further details. Once you have established yourself you can be so bold as to directly post your blog content. But remember that these must have value to the community for folk to interact with them and drive traffic to your content. And as always engage, carry your self well and respond to all comments.

Twitter

Advantages - URL from Twitter to external websites are permitted.

Twitter can be amazing or it can be a ghost town. If you regularly use the platform then choose Twitter as your main business platform. Again community is key, find the hashtags related to the problems you solve, and answer peoples problems, establish your self as an expert and link to your blogs, product and services. And as always engage, carry your self well and respond to all comments.

YouTube

Advantages - URLs from YouTube to external websites are permitted in the video description. Note: You must use https:// before your URL to make it active and clickable.

YouTube is a great place to house your videos as described earlier it is a Google product and gets indexed fast. I recommend making a video for every page and blog post you create and hosting that video on your page. Treat your description like your page header, use Keywords and use keywords in your tags.

<u>Strategies:</u>

1: Always brand your videos and have a strong call to action to push viewers to your website, to subscribe, to like and share.

2: A good strategy to get people to your videos/channel is to subscribe to all the key players in your industry. For the top five or so click the bell notification to be notified when their videos go live. Now, if these are the top players in your field, they are probably guaranteed to get lots of traffic so getting in first and leaving a comment can be a great way to push your content and encourage folks to check out your channel.

"Thanks for posting this, your explanation of why SEO is important is on point. You rock. Keep up the great work"

As this is one of the first comments it will get a number of likes and possibly a reply from the channel, in your reply leave a link to your content.

Tools

Use vidIQ Free account to see information about your videos and your competitor's videos. It gives your video an SEO score out of 100, shows the engagement rate, gives a video optimisation check list. Shows information about the channel and video like total views, avg daily views , subscribers in last 30 days, video tags for any video. This is a great tool to help you research and apply SEO practices to your YouTube videos.

https://vidiq.com/

Instagram

Only provides an external URL link from your profile and from posts for accounts with over 10K followers. However, this can be circumnavigated by creating a shop, then you can tag your products in each post. These shop products have links to your website. Products must be purchasable on your website for shop features to be approved. Alternatively add a service like later.com to allow you to link each image to an appropriate URL of your choice.

TikTok

Only provides an external URL link from your profile if you convert your profile to business. TikTok videos have a great chance of going viral.

Pinterest

Advantages - URL from Pinterest to external websites are permitted.

Great place to push images and videos. With each item uploaded you can link to your product or service. Sign up for the business account to get analytics.

LinkedIn

Advantages - URL from LinkedIn to external websites are permitted.

It is a strange platform, sorry I have no real experience here but it does allow external websites to be linked to so take advantage of it. As there is a culture of folks going to your profile to asses your expertise, experince etc. Make it straight to the point. By letting visitors know what you can do to help them and a link to your website.

Note: In my book Smartphone Smart Marketing, I go into more depth into Facebook, Twitter, Instagram and YouTube including social media strategies, content creation and distribution strategies.

https://www.robbwallace.co.uk/books/smartphone-smart-marketing/

Software

Check your Facebook, Pinterest and LinkedIn signals here. Use specific pages to see what kind of shares each has.

http://socialsignalscheck.com/

15

IMAGES

Images play such an important part of a brand's online presence. An image can convey a thousand words. Having a website means you will most definitely have images. They can make or break your website. The first WordPress website I built for my photography, I uploaded the images straight from my DSLR at full resolution, these images were up to 18 MB. As you can imagine my website was super slow. It took minutes to load. I had no idea! Learn from my early mistakes.

Compelling Images

Make sure your images are unique and make sure they are relevant and compelling. Don't just populate your website with hundreds of images for the sake of it. This will increase load times, every image must serve a purpose and must have its place. Use google image search to see how unique your images are. Be aware of using generic images from popular sites. Always take time to edit your images. You can edit them with free apps on your phone!

1: If Google sees that your images are the same as hundreds of other sites, it will devalue the content as it sees it as generic.

2: Users do the same, for example you click onto a gym website and the images are generic, not from that gym, just good looking models from some generic photography package. It does not build trust, makes you question, what are they hiding? Use your own compelling images.

Grab my book on Smartphone Smart Marketing to learn how to take great shots with your phone.

https://www.robbwallace.co.uk/books/smartphone-smart-marketing/ Sorry i keep on pushing my book, but if you need help learning how to market, create content etc it is a solid option. It is a part of my Layman's guide series.

Compress Your Images

Increase the speed and reduce the page weight by compressing your images. Using a software like Photoshop or Affinty photo to compress your images is a good start. I use https://shortpixel.com in the backend of my WordPress site to compress the images on the fly.

Formatted For The Medium

Shape, width, height and format. If your website is designed for mobile first experience you want to have a lot of square or 16:9 images as these will display best on a mobile screen. Very wide images may look good on an ultra wide desktop screen but they look terrible on a mobile phone. User experience!!

Follow Basic Photography Rules

If you are going to use your own images for your website, learn to use a camera. Understand the settings, and the rules of photography. For information on all of this including the settings and rules i.e 80/20, rule of thirds, perspective, ISO, shutter speed etc then grab a copy of https://www.robbwallace.co.uk/books/smartphone-smart-marketing/

Branded

Branding your images makes it harder for people to steal your images and no matter where they travel across the internet it allows potential viewers to find their way to your website.

Geo Tagged

If your product or service is location based, geo tag your images. This works well for both web images embedded on your website and images uploaded to your *Google My Business* account.

You can geo tag images by selecting the setting on modern phones and compact cameras with built in GPS. You can also use website like https://www.geoimgr.com/ to tag them.

16

VIDEO

Video plays such an important part of a brand's online presence and should be a major part of any and every marketing and SEO strategy.

Compelling Video

Does your website use video that improves the user experience by adding value? Are your videos up to the same standard as your other creative assets? Do they tell a story, provide reviews or how tos, etc? Take a minute to evaluate your videos and make sure that they are of value to those visiting your website.

Hosting Video.

The best way to host video on your website is to host them externally and use a lightbox with a single image which is lazy loaded (thumb nail) to represent the video. Then when the images is clicked, this is when the video begins to load. Embedding multiple or even just one YouTube video onto a page without using this method can dramatically reduce the speed of a website. Video is a data intensive medium and can increase the page weight or page ten fold.

17

Regularity

To build an online digital presence, you must play the long game. SEO is a dark art but it is not an instant art. As mentioned earlier, for instant SERP ranking use Google ads, for increased traffic over time we use SEO techniques. Hence why we must provide new and interesting content on a regular basis.

Regularity Of Blog Posts

Create a blog schedule in Google Docs, write down all the keywords you're targeting. Create ten blogs around each product or service and aim to write a blog about each of these topics weekly.

Consistency

Be consistent in your quality. It is easy to let the standard slip. Keep the content coming regularly and be accountable, keep your standard consistent. Your repeat customers or return visitors will notice a slip in quality.

Social Media Posts

Same as the blogs, keep them regular. This is why I encourage only advertising and populating networks you actually use. This way you don't get overwhelmed with attempting to create mountains of content.

Variety

For your own sanity and to create great engaging content for your customer base, incorporate variety into your creative schedule. Every so often mix it up, invite a guest blogger or reviewer, create an infographic, or just do something different. As they say, "variety is the spice of life." You never know who may read it! Avoid lots of repetitive content.

Update

Older blogs and pages will need updating. Products and services, address, prices, delivery information. Everything is always changing. For great customer experience make sure your information is up to date. This also looks good to Google, showing the website is updated and maintained.

Internal Links

Always make sure to link relevant keywords in your blogs to relevant "core" pages on your website. If I write a blog about marketing for authors I may highlight **Marketing Books** and link it to one of my marketing book pages. This is telling Google that this is not the main page on this topic and this is supporting my core content or pillar content i.e my product page.

18

EMAIL SUBSCRIPTION

A good way to nurture a prospective buyer. A good way to position your expertise and services. At the end of the day, we build a website to reach people be it for sales or what not. Newsletters are a tried and tested method for building an audience and driving traffic to your latest blog or product. However, running a bad newsletter campaign full of spam can drive an enthusiastic super fan away and even to the competition.

Sign Up

If you have a newsletter, can a customer sign up via your website? Is it easy to locate? Ask a friend to sign up and see if it is indeed easy to locate. If you're keen on building a newsletter make sure it is in the header, or footer and make it super obvious, with a clear call to action to encourage visitors to sign up.

Time To First Email

Test your system, how long is it till the customer receives their first email? Does this need adjusted?

Frequency Of Emails

Are you spamming folk straight of the bat? Are you sending out an initial email and then following up four months later? Look at the data, check the open rates. Make a plan and let your customers know the frequency they can expect. I follow two main newsletters, one promises tech news every morning and it delivers, and almost every morning I open it! The other promises world news stories weekly and it delivers, and 7 out of 10 I open and read. They don't spam, they are regular and they deliver. And because of this I read them, to me they are just like regular news channels on the TV or a paperboy delivering the daily newspaper. You know it is coming and you make time to read it..

Is The Content Of Value Or Just Sales?

Just like your blog and social content your newsletters have to be of value. They can't just be sales, sales, sales. Make a plan and deliver it.

Are They Spammy?

I hope note.

Easy To Unsubscribe

Make sure it is easy to unsubscribe. If the content is not worthy of your time, then making it easy to subscribe is good. When the bear is angry about our product or service we do not continue to poke the bear by making it a Mensa level maze to unsubscribe from the newsletter. If this happens to me I go out my way to make sure they know how unsatisfied I am with them. I am sure others do too.

19

Competitors

How do they fare? Make a list of all your competitors. I love to create a spreadsheet. Create a column for each of the topics below and anything else you deem relevant and this will hopefully bring a few fresh ideas to the table for how you can improve.

On Website User Experience

Set yourself a series of task to perform on each of the competitors' websites. Carry out the task on mobile and desktop.

Example: Sign up to their newsletter, add a product to cart, find the contact information, navigate to their key product type, read a blog etc Make notes on your experience, both good and bad and implement anything learned or needed to your own website.

On Product And Services

Compare the price, the images, video, words, keywords, content length, load speed, and everything else. Compile what you learn to make your site stronger.

On Keywords

Use SEO meta one click > Tool > Analyse Keyword density to get a flavour and measure of the keywords they are using and update your copy with any key ones you are missing.

On Reviews And Online Trust

Check their reviews. Check the ones they highlight on the website and the ones they have externally on sites like Google My Business, Amazon, Trustpilot , Feefo, Facebook etc. See what they do well and what they do bad in the eyes of the customers. Make a strategy to capitalise on their weakness and learn from their strengths.

On Social Media

See what channels they use. If all of your competitors are using the same channel, this could either be because it is the best or just that your industry has not branched out to other social networks. It may indicate that other channels are still to be mined! Take note of the regularity of content, types of content that is getting engagement, the adverts they run, the kind of comments they get. See what works and replicate it.

On PPC

Type your keywords into Google and see who is advertising. See what they are saying in their advert. Do you have a similar product? Is the advert worthy of copying and adapting? Now check https://www.similarweb.com and https://www.spyfu.com/ to see how much of the traffic to that keyword is via search and then how much of that is organic and how much is paid.

https://www.similarweb.com/

https://www.spyfu.com/

On Content

Is the quality of their content better or worse? Is their word count longer or shorter? Do they include custom graphics, appropriate videos and info graphics? Be honest when comparing your content and then bring yours up to the same standard or above.

On local Map Pack

Are they above you in the local map pack. Have a look through their GMB and see what you can learn. Check out the GMB Local section for more.

GMB & Local

This is Google's free business listing. Google loves Google, so make sure you don't miss out on this fantastic tool for local search traffic. Local SEO helps you target prospective customers in your business area. It's all about 'near me' with mobile searches. Your competitors may not focus on their Local SEO or GMB Performance. Even if you rank in the SERP, focusing on Local SEO & GMB SEO will complement your overall Organic SEO.

The main ranking factors for GMB are primary category, keywords in business title, proximity of search and positive Google reviews.

The Tool

https://software.easylocalcash.com this is an amazing tool for local searches. So let's hope it stays up. Type in your keyword, scroll on the map to your location, and click the map to drop a pin. Then hit search. Easy local cash will generate a table of results including:

Business name, Phone, Address, Citations, Google reviews, Keyword in business name, Average Star rating, Owner verified, Categories, Website, Tittle tag, pages indexed, Domain Authority, Backlinks.

A great tool for analysing the competition. As you can see this is a powerful tool.

GMB Claimed?

If you have a business up and running and you deliver a service locally, nationally or internationally *Google My Business* will probably have a listing ready for you to claim, if not, create one. Why? Because GMB gives you the ability to list your business location on Google maps and Google local search. GMB results often refer to the Map Pack or Local Pack, this is now the first thing displayed in SERPs when a local search is initiated. Try it, search for "plumber near me" or "*your business* near me". Claiming your GMB and linking it to your website is a strong indicator to Google that you are serious and will affect your local search rankings in a positive way. Now that you have claimed your GMB it is time to tick all the boxes!

Correct Address

You can provide GMB with your exact address or a service area depending on your business type. If you provide your address make sure it is correct and consistent. As mentioned earlier, when we populate our key information throughout the web we make sure that NAP is applied consistently. Name, Address, Phone number. NAP should be the same layout, spelling etc every time. And if you change your address years down the line, make sure you change your GMB and all your citations.

Category

You can select multiple categories, select as many as you need to convey what it is you do. However, the primary category is of utmost importance so choose the one closest to your service. Use the Easy local cash search to search your keyword and discover your competitor's category.

Contact Info

Make sure it is in the same format as every other NAP.

Google Messenger

It is worth signing up for it, as there is a GMB app and the message comes through to your phone.

Opening Times

Again consistency. Make sure these times are the same as your other listings and those advertised on your website, Facebook page, and local citation websites etc.

Reviews

Reviews are a ranking factor in GMB. Reviews tell Google and the customer about the quality you provide. Take some time and effort to secure good quality GMB reviews. Contact past customers, ask current customers and make a real effort to grow these.

Replies To Reviews

Reply to every review, again Google prompts you to do this, subtly telling you that this is important. When replying to reviews make sure you reference the Keywords and your

URL in reply. I.E *Thanks for reading my marketing book, much appreciated. Robb @ Robbwallace.co.uk*

This also goes for when you are leaving reviews. I make an effort to review every local business I interact with, leaving my URL in the review. i.e

Glasgow's best bakery. Grabbed two morning rolls with square sausage for a day full of meetings with clients. Gave me fuel for the day. robbwallace.co.uk recommends.

Images And Video

Your GMB listing has multiple categories for uploading images. Upload appropriate images and video for each category to gain engagement from folks looking at your listing. Note: Before uploading images, Geo tag them with your location, this adds another layer of information that tells Google that your business or service is local.

Posts, Offers, Events etc

Make a point of uploading a few posts a month, maybe not as regular as your main social channels but at least few posts a month.

Products And Services

Fill these in if you have products and services. Let your potential customers know.

Citations

Easy local cash and local Falcon as well as other tools show us that Google looks at the number of local citations you have listed as a ranking factor. Use my citations list to bolster your listings. Chapter 25.

Competition Average

Using Easy Local Cash or Google searches you can determine what you need to get to the top of the map pack. If you have filled in everything and are still being beaten in the map pack, look to make your website's domain strength i.e. your Domain Authority and your Backlink profile and follow the instruction in this book to make them stronger. Look at the averages and see what you need to pull up to be competitive.

Insights

GMB generates some good insights and data about how your customers interact and find your GMB listing and services. Study it and use that data to make your listing stronger.

Appears On The Map Pack With Keyword?

Test all of your keywords and questions that you would expect a map pack to return for and see what if any of yours make the map pack. Search "*business category*" near me, and test that as well. Are you n the map pack? Who is on the map pack?

NAP Clear On Website

Make sure your NAP is clear on your website.

Local Business

Make sure you are using the local business schema mark up on your website to let Google know you are a locally focused business.

Software

https://software.easylocalcash.com
www.localfalcon.com/

21

Analytics

There are many tools that allow you to measure your data. Demographics, time on site, landing pages, country of origin, traffic, traffic sources, devices and many, many more vital stats. Take time to install the appropriate tools to maximise the data from the traffic being generated from your website. Then learn how to analyse and understand that data. This will give you great insight into your website and what is working and what is not.

Google Search Console

As mentioned earlier a must for any new or exciting website.

Google Analytics

Again a must have if you are operating a website that you wish to rank on Google.

Other web analytics

There are many alternatives, some have heat maps that show you how customers navigate your site, others simplify the user interface of analytics. Most are expensive.

https://matomo.org/

https://oribi.io/

Facebook Pixel - Retargeting

If you are advertising on Facebook then you need to install a Facebook Pixel on your website. This bit of code will then track those leaving Facebook to your website and across the web, it is extremely powerful. It also delivers analytics about your website.

https://www.facebook.com/business/learn/facebook-ads-pixel

GMB Insights

Google My Business Insights gives all the analytics related to your GMB property.

Social Media Insights

Facebook, Twitter, YouTube, Instagram, Pinterest, TikTok all have analytic features which allows you to see how your audience is interacting with your content. Look at it, analyse it and see what is engaging, what content is getting people clicking, sharing, liking etc There is a wealth of data to be analysed from social.

22

REVIEWS

What are your prospective customers reading about your business? It is good to have a look at your reviews and see what gems can be found. Excellent reviews can be used on your website to build trust and help people make the buying decision. Bad reviews allow you to see where your gaps are and how you can improve. As always I would recommend going through your competitor's reviews as well. When asking customers for reviews I always ask them to mention the service in the review, another way to get a cheeky keyword in there.

Online Review Overview

Do an audit of all your online reviews. Timestamp which platforms and how many reviews each has. Set yourself some goals to increase your reviews. This can be a ranking factor on platforms like Google My Business.

Platforms

What platforms are you accepting reviews on? Which platform are your customers or users naturally drawn to? Which platform are you pushing and actively trying to grow?

Review Replies

Make sure to leave a review, take the time to say thank you to your customers who took the time to leave you a review. Also another opportunity to get a keyword or two in there.

How Do They Get Reviews?

What is your current strategy for getting reviews? Do not be shy in asking your customers or users to leave a review. Reviews are integral to business and customer trust. So make sure you ask and make sure you have a plan for getting reviews.

23

List of Software & Websites

Software and Tools

Software and websites specific to the task have been highlighted in each respective chapter. Here is a list of some that I may not have mentioned and some that I already have.

SEO Software

Some are free, some offer free trial, some are paid. Most offer everything from research, on page audits, technical audits, keyword research, competitor research and more

https://robb.link/SERPstat

https://robb.link/SEranking

https://www.alliai.com

https://www.seotesteronline.com

https://www.semrush.com

https://ahrefs.com

https://moz.com/products/pro

https://neilpatel.com/ubersuggest/

https://www.spyfu.com

https://www.woorank.com

https://www.seoptimer.com

https://website.grader.com

https://seekmetrics.com

https://seolyzer.io

https://www.screamingfrog.co.uk/seo-spider/

https://technicalseo.com/tools/

www.brokenlinkcheck.com

Local SEO

https://software.easylocalcash.com

Website Overview

http://nibbler.silktide.com

https://www.w3snoop.com

Content Writing

https://robb.link/ProWritingAid

https://www.frase.io

https://robb.link/rytr

https://answerthepublic.com

How Is A Website Built?

https://www.wpthemedetector.com

https://builtwith.com

https://www.wappalyzer.com

https://w3techs.com/sites/info

https://whatcms.org

https://wpbuffs.com/wordpress-plugin-theme-checkers/

Who Is Info

https://www.whois.com/whois

https://who.is/whois

Page Authority

https://www.seoreviewtools.com/website-authority-checker/

https://websiteseochecker.com/domain-authority-checker

https://smallseotools.com/alexa-rank-checker/

Speed

https://gtmetrix.com

https://tools.pingdom.com

https://www.uptrends.com/tools/website-speed-test

Websites

https://robb.link/SiteGround

https://robb.link/GeneratePress

Social Media Scheduling

https://sociality.io

Facebook Ads Spy

https://www.facebook.com/ads/library

Notes

trello.com

Great SEO Blogs

https://moz.com/blog
https://backlinko.com/blog
https://neilpatel.com/blog/
https://ahrefs.com/blog/
https://seranking.com/blog/
https://serpstat.com/blog/
https://www.semrush.com/blog/
https://searchengineland.com/
https://www.localseoguide.com/blog/
https://www.matthewwoodward.co.uk
https://www.craigcampbellseo.com/category/news/

Interesting Individuals

Rand Fishkin
https://twitter.com/randfish
Vanessa Fox
https://twitter.com/vanessafox
Danny Sulivan
https://twitter.com/dannysullivan
Brian Dean
https://twitter.com/Backlinko
Craig Campbell
twitter.com/craigcampbell03
Steven Kang
https://twitter.com/SEOSignalsLab

Facebook Groups

https://www.facebook.com/groups/SEOSignalsLab/

Marketplaces

appsumo.com

www.legiit.com

Google Search Functions - Search Operators

Related:robbwallace.co.uk

Link:robbwallace.co.uk

Site:robbwallace.co.uk

Inanchor:"marketing"

Inurl:keyword

Cache:robbwallace.co.uk

Keyword site:.com - searches all .com sites for that keyword- good for competition

Keyword site:robbwallace.co.uk - searches just rWM for that keyword.

"robbwallace.co.uk"

24

LIST OF CHROME PLUGINS

SEO Meta 1 Click

The swiss army knife of SEO plugins.

https://chrome.google.com/webstore/detail/seo-meta-in-1-click/bjogjfinolnhfhkbipphpdlldadpnmhc?hl=en

SEO Minion

Good for overview of SEO, and checking links (Broken links, 404s, redirects etc) on any website.

https://chrome.google.com/webstore/detail/seo-minion/giihipjfimkajhlcilipnjeohabimjhi

SEOstack Keyword Tool

Put in a keyword and it spits out hundreds.

https://chrome.google.com/webstore/detail/seostack-keyword-tool/labjajhkfjfncpiddbgdimcaldgeognn?hl=en

Text Optimizer

A brilliant extension that scans your website and scores your keywords. It then suggests keywords that you are missing in relation to your content.

https://chrome.google.com/webstore/detail/textoptimizer/fdbbkmpdjmpnebmdgbhcodhlafiicnkd/related

KeyWord Surfer

Gives you search volume directly in the Google search bar. Great for keyword research.

https://chrome.google.com/webstore/detail/keyword-surfer/bafijghppfhdpldihckdcadbcobikaca

Search Simulator By Nightwatch

Allows you to simulate Google searches in different locations and languages. Powerful

https://chrome.google.com/webstore/detail/seo-search-simulator-by-n/edfjfgjklednkencfhnokmkajbgfhpon/related?hl=en

Similar Webs - Traffic Rank & Website Analysis

Similar webs powerful tools in a chrome extension.

https://chrome.google.com/webstore/detail/similarweb-traffic-rank-w/hoklmmgfnpapgjgcpechhaamimifchmp/related?hl=en

Vid I Q

SEO for YouTube extension.

https://chrome.google.com/webstore/detail/vidiq-vision-for-youtube/pachckjkecffpdphbpmfolblodfkgbhl?hl=en

SerpStat

Great tool, works best with a subscription to SerpStat.

https://chrome.google.com/webstore/detail/serpstat-website-seo-chec/fcgbopaomlpldhbinhgebmkcnkfconmn?hl=en

25

List of Citations/ Profiles

Citations list

Business Directories And Listings UK

Sign up, verify your email, create a page and populate it with your brand logo, web URL, NAP and basic information. Is your business listed consistently. The only thing to change up between listings is your description, try different keywords associated with your main keyword etc. Different descriptions in etc.

business.google.com
directory.dailyrecord.co.uk
directory.independent.co.uk
facebook.com
foursquare.com
mapsconnect.apple.com
yell.com
yelp.com
2findlocal.com
communitywalk.com
cylex-uk.co.uk
ibegin.com
scoot.co.uk
spoke.com
thomsonlocal.com
tupalo.com
uksmallbusinessdirectory.co.uk
where2go.com
118information.co.uk

192.com
bingplaces.com
centralindex.com
freeindex.co.uk
hotfrog.co.uk
infobel.com
lacartes.com
touchlocal.com
brownbook.net
cityvisitor.co.uk
fyple.co.uk
mylocalservices.co.uk
thebestof.co.uk
thetradefinder.co.uk
tipped.co.uk
uk.bizadee.com
uk.myhuckleberry.com
www.misterwhat.co.uk
cybo.com

Business Directories and Listings USA

business.google.com
bingplaces.com
facebook.com
foursquare.com
mapquest.com
mapsconnect.apple.com
yellowpages.com
2findlocal.com
communitywalk.com
cybo.com
hotfrog.com
manta.com
merchantcircle.com
showmelocal.com
tupalo.com

where2go.com
yellowbook.com
chamberofcommerce.com
ezlocal.com
lacartes.com
local.com
mapquest.com
search.yahoo.com
spoke.com
bbb.org/en/us
bizvotes.com
brownbook.net
citysquares.com
elocal.com
getfave.com
insiderpages.com
local.botw.org
opendi.nl
tuugo.us
b2byellowpages.com
threebestrated.com

Profiles

Sign up, verify your email, create a page and populate it with your brand logo, web URL and basic information.

Facebook.com
Instagram.com
YouTube.com
LinkedIn.com
Twitter.com
Pintrest.com
TikTok.com
Myspace.com
Flickr.com
Vimeo.com

Skype.com

Reddit.com

Quora.com

slideshare.net

nextdoor.co.uk

www.xing.com/en

scribd.com

Meetup.com

www.deviantart.com

folio.procreate.art/showcase

Soundcloud.com

Ravelry.com

Goodreads.com

Behance.net

Blogger.com

Bloglovin.com

Reverbnation.com

Twitch.tv

Allrecipes.com

Flipboard.com

Medium.com

Bizsugar.com

wordpress.com

amazon.com/profile

livejournal.com

github.com

en.gravatar.com

issuu.com

imgur.com

etsy.com

disqus.com

archive.org

wix.com

kickstarter.com

ted.com

openstreetmap.org

tasks.hotosm.org

wiki.openstreetmap.org/wiki/Main_Page

about.me

last.fm

500px.com

crunchbase.com

boredpanda.com

wattpad.com

8tracks.com

moz.com/community

forums.envato.com

pearltrees.com

spreaker.com

anchor.fm

bookcrossing.com

magcloud.com

archilovers.com

stocktwits.com

knowem.com

community.growthhackers.com

lightstalking.com

www.academia.edu

buzzfeed.com

cafebabel.com

mix.com

ello.co

www.kiva.org

www.viki.com

triberr.com

tripadvisor.co.uk

tripadvisor.com

coub.com

ask.fm

26

ACTION PLAN FOR WEBSITE

So you've read through almost everything and you have implemented things here and there. I will assume you have had many "Ah-Ha" moments and that you are ready to get into the meat and two veg of SEO. You may also have had moments where you realised how complicated a solid SEO plan and the effort needed to put it into action can be. Don't worry I have a simple, step by step action plan to help you cover the basics.

Step one run an SEO audit of your website via one of the suggested Free or Paid options. Analyse what it returns and make improvements.

1. Keyword Research

Analyse your keywords

Analyse competitor keywords

Make a keyword list and plan for each page.

2. Website Optimization

Add your website Google Analytics

Add your website to Google Search Console

Register a local business on Google Maps

Create a logical site structure

Secure your website (HTTPS) with a SSL certificate

Define the preferred domain (www or non-www)

Create a robots.txt file

Create an XML sitemap

Create SEO-friendly URLs

Use breadcrumb navigation

Create user-friendly interlinking

Set up a 404 page

Use Canonical URL

Fix broken links

Mind the number of outbound links

Improve each pages load speed

Compress images

Lazy load images and video

Reduce page size

Reduce requests

Use a CDN

3. User Experience

Make your website responsive and mobile friendly

Make your message clear

Make your website easy to navigate.

Make it Fat Finger friendly (buttons, forms and menus)

Always on top menus

Contrast and colours

4. Content Strategy

Write a unique title for each page

Write a unique meta description for each page

Optimise H-tags (heading tags with your keywords, only one H1 per page.)

Use alt tags in every image

Optimise content both for robots and humans

Know your audience, know your brand

Develop a content plan

Add a blog to your website

Create value with your content

Create fresh, relevant content

5. Backlinks and Citations

Analyse your competitors' backlink profiles

Create a link-building strategy

Create social profiles

Create citations

Create Press Releases

Cooperate with websites by sharing relevant content within the niche

Participate in niche forum discussions and answer the questions (Quora, Reddit, etc.)

Guest post

Encourage users to write reviews about your product or service

Use images, videos, and documents for website promotion

6: Social Media Strategy

Check the social signals

Create lots of regular content

Add social media buttons to your website

Add share buttons

Use the Open Graph protocol for social media posts

27

Conclusion

Now you are ready to become an SEO warrior, well at least start your journey with the mindset of an SEO warrior. However, knowledge is not power, the application of knowledge is power. You will not be able to implement everything in this book. You will never get 100% speed scores or 100 out of 100 on an SEO audit from one of the suggested SEO software packages. However, you can make plans, and implement a little at a time and make your website progressively better over time and as you do, your site will rank higher and higher. Continuous grind!!

If you enjoyed this book in any way, please leave a review on the platform you purchased it from. It makes a huge difference. If you have a website, please feel free to send a backlink to my book at https://www.robbwallace.co.uk/books/seo-a-laymans-guide/

If you do leave a review let me know at authorrobb@gmail.com, send me a pic, a link to the review and your website and I will give you a backlink from the books page.

For more books check out https://www.robbwallace.co.uk/ and feel free to hit me up on social.

Thanks for reading.

Here is to your success.

Robb

Made in the USA
Monee, IL
04 November 2026

67377200R00066